AF600628

E APOSTOLIC CONSTITUTION
CHRISTUS DOMINUS:

XT, TRANSLATION AND COMMENTARY, WITH
ORT ANNOTATIONS ON THE MOTU PROPRIO
SACRAM COMMUNIONEM

he Apostolic Constitution *Christus Dominus:*

xt, Translation and Commentary, with short anno-
ions on the Motu Proprio *Sacram Communionem*

A DISSERTATION

Submitted to the Faculty of the School of Canon Law of the Catholic University of America in Partial Fulfillment of the Requirements for the Degree of Doctor of Canon Law

BY THE

REV. JAMES RUDDY, J.C.L.
Priest of the Diocese of Cheyenne

E CATHOLIC UNIVERSITY OF AMERICA PRESS
WASHINGTON, D. C.

Nihil Obstat:

CLEMENS V. BASTNAGEL, S.T.L., J.U.D.,
Censor Deputatus.

Washingtonii, die 17 maii, 1957.

Imprimatur:

✠ HUBERT M. NEWELL, D.D.,
Episcopus Cheyennensis.

Cheyennensi, die 20 maii, 1957.

Printed by
THE WICKERSHAM PRINTING CO.
Lancaster, Penna.

DEDICATED TO THE MEMORY OF

MY FATHER AND MOTHER

FOREWORD *

WITH THE promulgation of the Apostolic Constitution *Christus Dominus* on January 6, 1953, came the most far-reaching changes in the law of the Eucharistic Fast since Apostolic times. These changes were the completion of a policy begun more than half a century ago when Pope St. Pius X issued through the Sacred Congregation of the Council the decree *Post editum* of December 7, 1906, which enabled the sick to receive Holy Communion without the complete observance of the natural fast. This relaxation of the law was later embodied in the Code of Canon Law. Since the promulgation of the Code further relaxations and dispensations from the obligation of the law were granted particularly to the armed forces and to war workers during the second world war. Because these relaxations were of a temporary nature and confined to certain classes of people they were not sufficient to enable all who desired to receive Holy Communion frequently to conveniently do so. Consequently, it was to be expected that a unifying law to fit all circumstances would eventually be promulgated. This has been accomplished through the new Eucharistic legislation.

Since the promulgation of the new law many problems have arisen and canonists have by no means been unanimous in their solution. The purpose of this work is to endeavor to contribute to a uniformity of practice in the application of the principles as set down in the new legislation.

The writer does not however, attempt to treat all the problems; he has made an effort simply to give his solution of the

* The present work was undertaken without any knowledge of the recent change in the legislation on the Eucharistic fast and evening Masses. Before its completion, however, the Motu Proprio *Sacram Communionem* of Pius XII abrogated the law decreed in the Apostolic Constitution *Christus Dominus,* and supplanted it with a more recent one. The writer therefore has added an appendix on the new legislation giving the text, translation and a short commentary on the same.

more practical ones. Undoubtedly, as time goes on, official responses will clarify these problems, but in the meantime canonists are free to interpret the law according to the norms of interpretation found in the Code and in the Instruction of the Sacred Congregation of the Holy Office of January 6, 1953, which is the authentic interpretation of the Apostolic Constitution.

The translation of the Apostolic Constitution *Christus Dominus* and of the concomitant Instruction of the Sacred Congregation of the Holy Office is reproduced from the work of the Reverend John C. Ford, S.J., entitled *The New Eucharistic Legislation*. The writer wishes to thank P. J. Kenedy and Sons, publishers and copyright holders of the same, through whose courtesy this translation is used.

The writer welcomes this opportunity to express his sincere gratitude to His Excellency, the Most Reverend Hubert M. Newell, D.D., Bishop of Cheyenne, for the opportunity of advanced study in the School of Canon Law at the Catholic University of America. The writer wishes also to thank the Reverend Clement V Bastnagel, J.U.D., for his generous and scholarly direction, the Faculty of the School of Canon Law for their kind encouragement, and all others for their helpful suggestions, all of which together have made this dissertation possible.

TABLE OF CONTENTS

CHAPTER IV

CHAPTER V

CHAPTER VI

APPENDIX

THE MOTU PROPRIO *SACRAM COMMUNIONEM*

PART I

TEXT AND TRANSLATION

CONSTITUTIO APOSTOLICA*

De Disciplina Servanda Quoad Ieiunium Eucharisticum

PIUS EPISCOPUS

Servus Servorum Dei
Ad Perpetuam Rei Memoriam

(1) Christus Dominus, "in qua nocte tradebatur",[1] cum postrema vice veteris Legis celebravit Pascha, coena facta,[2] accepit panem, et gratias agens fregit, deditque discipulis suis dicens: "Hoc est corpus meum, quod pro vobis tradetur",[3] itemque calicem eis porrexit asseverans: "Hic est sanguis meus novi testamenti, qui pro multis effundetur",[4] "Hoc facite in meam commemorationem".[5] Quibus ex Sacrarum Litterarum locis omnino patet Divinum Redemptorem ultimae huic paschali celebrationi, in qua agnus ex Hebraeorum ritibus manducabatur, voluisse substituere novum Pascha, ad saeculorum usque obitum permansurum, esum videlicet immaculati Agni, immolandi pro mundi vita, ita ut novum Pascha novae Legis Phase vetus terminaret, et umbram fugaret veritas.[6]

(2) Quandoquidem autem utriusque coenae euismodi coniunctio idcirco habita fuit, ut ex antiquo Paschate ad novum significaretur transitus, facile perspici potest cur Ecclesia, in Eucharistico Sacrificio ex Divini Redemptoris iussu in eius commemorationem renovando, a veteris agapes more discedere potuerit, et Eucharisticum ieiunium in usum inducere.

(3) Etenim inde ab antiquissima aetate consuetudo invaluit

* Ex Commentario *Acta Apostolicae Sedis,* n. 1, die 16 Ianuarii 1953 edito, Vol. XXXXV (Ser. II, v. XX), N.I.

1 *I Cor.,* XI, 23.

2 Cfr. Luc., XXII, 20.

3 *I Cor.,* XI, 24.

4 Matth., XXVI, 28

5 Cfr. *I Cor.,* XI, 24-25.

6 Cfr. hymn. *Lauda Sion* (Missale Rom.).

APOSTOLIC CONSTITUTION

On the Discipline to be Observed Concerning the Eucharistic Fast

PIUS, BISHOP

Servant of the Servants of God
For an Everlasting Remembrance

(1) Christ the Lord, on the "night in which He was betrayed," * when for the last time He celebrated the Pasch of the Old Law, took bread, and, giving thinks, broke, and gave to His disciples, after supper was finished, saying: "This is My body which shall be delivered for you"; and in the same way He handed the chalice to them with the words: "This do in commemoration of Me." These passages of Holy Scripture are clear evidence that Our Divine Redeemer wanted to substitute for that final paschal celebration, in which a lamb was eaten according to the Hebrew rite, a new Pasch to endure till the end of the world; namely, the eating of the immaculate Lamb, who was to be immolated for the life of the world, so that the new Pasch of the New Law brought the ancient Passover to an end, and truth dispelled the shadow.

(2) But since the relationship of the two suppers was brought about to signify the transition from the old Pasch to the new, it is easy to see why the Church, in renewing the Eucharistic Sacrifice by command of the Divine Redeemer and in commemoration of Him, could relinquish the custom of the ancient love feast, and introduce the practice of the Eucharistic fast.

(3) From the very earliest times the custom developed of administering the Eucharist to the faithful fasting. About the end

Eucharistiam christifidelibus ieiunis administrandi.[7] Saeculo autem exeunte quarto iam in variis Conciliis ieiunium iis praecipiebatur, qui Eucharisticum celebraturi essent Sacrificium. Itaque anno CCCLXXXXIII Hipponense Concilium haec decrevit: "Sacramenta altaris non nisi a ieiunis hominibus celebrentur"; [8] quod praeceptum paulo post, hoc est anno CCCLXXXXVII, ex Carthaginensi Concilio III iisdem verbis edebatur; [9] ac saeculo ineunte quinto haec consuetudo satis communis et immemorabilis dici potest; quamobrem S. Augustinus affirmat sanctissimam Eucharistiam a ieiunis semper accipi itemque per universum orbem morem istum servari.[10]

(4) Procul dubio haec agendi ratio gravissimis innitebatur causis, in quibus ea ante omnia memorari potest, quam Apostolus gentium lamentatur, cum de fraterna christianorum agape agit.[11] Etenim cibo potuque se abstinere cum summa illa reverentia congruit, quam supremae Iesu Christi maiestati debemus, cum eum Eucharisticis delitescentem velis sumpturi sumus. Ac praeterea, dum, ante quodlibet alimentum, eius pretiosissimo Corpore ac Sanguine vescimur, luculenter demonstramus illud esse primum ac summum nutrimentum, quo animus alatur noster eiusque augeatur sanctitas. Quapropter idem Augustinus haec monet: "Placuit Spiritui Sancto ut in honorem tanti Sacramenti in os christiani prius Dominicum Corpus intraret quam ceteri cibi".[12]

(5) Neque debitum solummodo honoris munus hoc ieiunium Divino tribuit Redemptori, sed pietatem etiam fovet; ideoque ad saluberrimos illos sanctitatis fructus augendos conferre potest, quos bonorum omnium fons et auctor Christus a nobis, gratia ditatis, elici postulat.

(6) Nemo ceteroquin est, qui experiundo non agnoscat ex ipsis humanae naturae legibus contingere ut, cum corpus cibo oneratum non sit, mens erigatur agilior, atque impensiore moveatur

[7] Cfr. Ben. XIV, *De Syn. Dioec.*, L. 6, c. 8, n. 10.

[8] Conc. Hipp., can. 28: Mansi, III, 923.

[9] Conc. Carth. III, cap. 29: Mansi, III, 885.

[10] Cfr. S. August., *Ep. LIV ad Ian.*, cap. 6: Migne, *PL*, XXXIII, 203.

[11] Cfr. *I Cor.*, XI, 21 sq.

[12] S. August., l.c.

of the fourth century fasting was prescribed by several Councils for those who were going to celebrate the Eucharistic Sacrifice. Thus in the year 393 the Council of Hippo decreed: "Let the Sacrament of the Altar be celebrated only by those who are fasting." Soon after, in the year 397, the same prescription was made by the Third Council of Carthage in the very same words; and by the beginning of the fifth century this custom was sufficiently common to be called immemorial. Hence St. Augustine affirms that the most Holy Eucharist was always received fasting and also that this usage was observed throughout the world.

(4) Doubtless this practice was based on very serious reasons, among which may be mentioned first of all the situation deplored by the Apostle of the Gentiles when he deals with the fraternal love feast of the Christians. For to abstain from food and drink is in keeping with that deep reverence which we owe to the supreme majesty of Jesus Christ, when we are about to receive Him hidden under the Eucharistic veils. And furthermore, when we consume His most precious body and blood before any other food, we give clear evidence that this is the first and most excellent nourishment, by which the soul is sustained and its holiness increased. That is why St. Augustine reminds us: "It has seemed good to the Holy Ghost, that in honor of so great a sacrament the body of the Lord should enter into the mouth of a Christian before any other food."

(5) Nor does this fast merely pay a tribute of honor, due to the Divine Redeemer. It also fosters devotion. And accordingly it can help to increase those salutary fruits of holiness, which Christ, the fountain and author of all good things, requires us who are enriched by His grace to bring forth.

(6) Besides, who does not know from experience of the very laws of human nature that when the body is not burdened with food, the mind reacts with more agility and is inspired to meditate

virtute ad arcanum illud excelsumque meditandum mysterium, quod in animo, tamquam in templo, agitur, divinam adaugens caritatem.

(7) Quanta cura Ecclesia Eucharisticum ieiunium servandum curaverit ex eo etiam erui potest, quod illud, gravibus quoque poenis violatoribus impositis, imperavit. Etenim Concilium Toletanum VII, anno DCXXXXVI, excommunicationem ei comminatum est, qui non ieiunus sacris fuisset operatus,[13] anno autem DLXXII Concilium Bracarense III,[14] et anno DLXXXV Concilium Matisconense II [15] iam decreverant eum, qui huius rei evasisset reus, de sui muneris honorisque sede deponendum esse.

(8) Attamen, volventibus saeculis, illud quoque diligenter consideratum est, interdum nempe esse opportunum, ob peculiaria rerum adiuncta, hanc ieiunii legem, ad christifideles quod attinet, aliquatenus relaxare. Quam ad rem Constantiae Concilium, anno MCCCXV, dum eiusmodi sacrosanctam legem confirmat, addit quoque quoddam temperamentum: ". . . sacrorum canonum auctoritas, laudabilis et approbata consuetudo Ecclesiae servavit et servat, quod huiusmodi sacramentum non debet confici post coenam, neque a fidelibus recipi non ieiunis, nisi in casu infirmitatis aut alterius necessitatis a iure vel Ecclesia concesso vel admisso ".[16]

(9) Placuit haec in memoriam ea de causa reducere, ut omnes perspectum habeant Nos, quamvis novae temporum rerumque condiciones suadeant ut non paucas facultates ac venias hac in re concedamus, velle tamen per Apostolicas has Litteras summam huius legis consuetudinisque vim confirmare ad Eucharisticum quod attinet ieiunium; ac velle etiam eos admonere, qui eidem legi obtemperare queant, ut id facere pergant diligenter, ita quidem ut ii solummodo, qui in necessitate versentur, hisce concessionibus frui possint secundum eiusdem necessitatis rationes.

(10) Suavissimo Nos solacio afficimur—quod libet heic, etsi breviter, declarare—cum pietatem cernimus erga Augustum altaris Sacramentum cotidie magis increbrescere non modo in christifidelium animis, sed ad divini cultus etiam splendorem

[13] Conc. Tolet. VII, cap. 2: Mansi, X, 768.

[14] Conc. Bracar. III, can. 10: Mansi, IX, 841.

[15] Conc. Matiscon. II, can. 6: Mansi, IX, 952.

[16] Conc. Constant., sess. XIII: Mansi, XXVII, 727.

with greater fervor on that hidden and sublime mystery which is enacted in the temple of the soul to the increase of divine charity.

(7) The solicitude with which the Church watches over the observance of the Eucharistic fast may be gathered also from this, that she commanded this fast under severe penalties against its violators. Thus the Seventh Council of Toledo in the year 646 threatened with excommunication anyone who had said Mass not fasting; while in the year 572 the Third Council of Braga, and in the year 585 the Second Council of Macon had already decreed that anyone who incurred this guilt should be deprived of his dignities and deposed from office.

(8) As the centuries passed, however, careful consideration was given to the fact that sometimes it was expedient, because of special circumstances, to relax somewhat this law of fasting as regards the faithful. For this reason the Council of Constance in the year 1415, while reaffirming the sacrosanct law of the fast, added a certain qualification: ". . . the authority of the sacred canons, together with the praiseworthy, authorized usage of the Church, has maintained and does maintain that this sacrament should not be celebrated after supper, nor should it be received by the faithful not fasting, except in a case of sickness, or in a case of other necessity recognized by law or permitted by the Chruch."

(9) It has seemed good to recall these facts to mind in order that all may recognize that We, although induced by the new conditions of affairs and of the times to grant not a few faculties and permissions in this matter, intend, nevertheless, by these Apostolic Letters to retain in full force the law and custom respecting the Eucharistic fast; and We wish, furthermore, to remind those who are able to obey this law, that they continue diligently to do so, so that only those who are in necessity may enjoy these concessions, according to the measure of that necessity.

(10) We are filled with the sweetest consolation—and We are glad to mention it here, if only briefly—when We perceive that devotion to the August Sacrament of the Altar is on the increase day by day, not only in the souls of the faithful, but also as regards the splendor of divine worship which time and again shines

quod pertinet, qui ex publicis populorum manifestationibus saepenumero emicat. Quam ad rem haud parum procul dubio contulere sollicitae Summorum Pontificum curae, ac praesertim Beati Pii X, qui quidem, ad priscam Ecclesiae consuetudinem renovandam omnes advocans, eos adhortatus est, ut quam creberrime, immo cotidie si possent, ad Angelorum mensam accederent; [17] ac parvulos quoque ad caeleste hoc pabulum invitans, sapienti consilio statuit praeceptum sacrae Confessionis sacraeque Communionis ad eos singulos universos spectare, qui iam ad rationis usum pervenissent; [18] quod etiam in iuris canonici Codice sancitum est.[19] Hisce Summorum Pontificum curis christifideles ultro libenterque respondentes, ad sacram Synaxim frequentiores usque accessere. Atque utinam haec caelestis Panis fames divinique Sanguinis sitis in omnibus cuiusvis aetatis hominibus in omnibusque civium ordinibus exardescant!

(11) Animadvertendum tamen est ea quibus vivimus tempora eorumque peculiares condiciones multa in societatis usum in communisque vitae actionem induxisse, ex quibus graves difficultates oriantur, quae possint homines a divinis participandis mysteriis abstrahere, si Eucharistici ieiunii legi eo prorsus modo ab omnibus obtemperandum sit, quo ad praesens usque tempus obtemperandum erat.

(12) Imprimisque patet omnibus clerum hodie ingravescentibus christianorum necessitatibus numero imparem esse; qui quidem festis praesertim diebus nimium saepe laborem tolerare debet, cum serius Eucharisticum Sacrificium ac non raro etiam bis vel ter celebrare debeat, cumque interdum officio quoque teneatur longinquum faciendi iter, ut sacra ne desint haud parvis sui gregis partibus. Enervantes eiusmodi apostolici labores sacerdotum valetudinem procul dubio debilitant; idque eo vel magis quod non modo Missae litandae cum Evangelii explicatione, itemque sacris Confessionibus audiendis, catechesi impertiendae, ceterisque sui muneris partibus increscenti studio increscentique

[17] S. Congr. Concilii, Decretum *Sacra Tridentina Synodus,* d. d. xx mensis Decembris, an. MCMV: *Acta S. Sedis,* XXXVIII, 400 sq.

[18] S. Congr. de Sacramentis, Decretum *Quam singulari,* d. d. VIII mensis Augusti, an MCMX: *Acta Ap. Sedis,* II, 577 sq.

[19] C.I.C., can. 863; cfr. can. 854, § 5.

forth in public demonstrations by the people. The paternal directives of the Sovereign Pontiffs have doubtless contributed no little to this result. This is particularly true of Blessed Pius X, who called upon all to revive the primitive usage of the Church, exhorting them to receive the Bread of Angels very frequently, and even daily if possible; and inviting children, too, to this heavenly food, he wisely decreed that the precept of Confession and Holy Communion pertained to each and every one who had reached the use of reason; and this prescription was confirmed in the Code of Canon Law. In generous and willing response to these directives of the Sovereign Pontiffs the faithful have approached the Holy Table in ever increasing numbers. And would that this hunger for the Bread of Heaven and thirst for the divine Blood might burst into flame among all men, whatever their age or social station may be!

(11) Yet it must be noted that the peculiar conditions of the times in which we live have introduced many changes into the usages of society and the practices of everyday life. This gives rise to serious difficulties which can prevent people from taking part in the divine mysteries, if they all have to obey the law of the Eucharistic fast exactly as it had to be obeyed up to the present.

(12) In the first place, it is obvious to everyone that the clergy today are not sufficiently numerous to meet the ever more burdensome needs of Christians. Especially on holy days they are often overburdened with labors, because they must celebrate the Eucharistic Sacrifice at a late hour, and frequently even twice or three times, and also because at times it is their duty to make a long journey in order that large sections of their flock may not be deprived of Mass. Exhausting apostolic labors of this kind undoubtedly weaken the health of priests; and this all the more because besides saying Mass and explaining the Gospel, hearing confessions, teaching catechism, taking care of the other duties of

opera vacare debent, sed iis etiam rationibus rebusque diligenter prospicere ac consulere, quas asperum illud certamen adversus Deum eiusque Ecclesiam postulat, tam late hodie, tam callide acriterque excitatum.

(13) At mens animusque noster ad eos potissimum advolat, qui procul a patria cuiusque sua, in longinquis operantes terris, huic Divini Magistri invitationi iussionique generosi responderunt: " Euntes ergo docete omnes gentes "; [20] ad Evangelii praecones dicimus, qui, gravissimis etiam exantlatis laboribus atque itinerum difficultatibus omne genus superatis, eo omni nisu contendunt, ut christianae religionis lumen omnibus pro facultate affulgeat, utque suos greges, saepenumero a catholica suscepta fide adhuc recentes, angelico illo enutriant cibo, qui virtutem alat pietatemque refoveat.

(14) Iisdem fere in rerum adiunctis ii quoque christifideles versantur, qui vel in non paucis regionibus a catholicis Missionalibus excultis, vel in aliis locis commorantes, cum proprium apud se non habeant sacrorum administrum, alterius sacerdotis adventum in seras horas exspectare debent, ut Eucharisticum participare queant Sacrificium, seseque divino enutrire pabulo.

(15) Ac praeterea, postquam machinae omne genus in usum inductae fuere, saepissime contingit ut opifices non pauci vel officinis, vel vehicularibus maritimisque muneribus, vel aliis publicae utilitatis officiis addicti, non modo per diem sed per noctem etiam alternis iteratisque laboris vicibus occupentur, ita quidem ut debilitatae eorum vires eos interdum compellere possint ad aliquid nutrimenti accipiendum, atque adeo iidem impediantur quominus ad Eucharisticam mensam ieiuni accedant.

(16) Ad hanc eamdem mensam matres quoque familias saepenumero venire nequeunt, antequam domesticis curis prospexerint, quae multas saepe ab eis postulant laboris horas.

(17) Parique modo evenit ut in puerorum puellarumque scholis ac litterarum ludis plurimi habeantur, qui divino illi invitamento respondere cupiant: " Sinite parvulos venire ad me " [21] cum fore omnino confidant ut ille, qui " pascitur inter lilia " [22] suum

[20] Matth., XXVIII, 19.

[21] Marc., X, 14.

[22] *Cant.*, II, 16; VI, 2.

their office with more and more effort, more and more toil, they must, in addition, be diligently on the lookout to provide those measures which are demanded by the relentless warfare which in our day has been launched so artfully, so bitterly, and on so many fronts against God and His Church.

(13) But our mind and heart go out most of all to those who are laboring in distant countries, far from their native land, obeying generously the invitation and command of the Divine Master: " Going, therefore, teach ye all nations "; We refer to the heralds of the Gospel, who, enduring the heaviest toil, and overcoming all kinds of obstacles in their journeys, bend every effort that the light of the Christian religion may dawn for all men as far as in them lies, and that their flocks, many of whom are but recently received into the Catholic faith, may be nourished by that Angelic food which fosters virtue and rekindles devotion.

(14) In almost the same circumstances are those Christians who live in the many regions cared for by Catholic missionaries, or in other localities, but who, since they do not have a resident priest, must wait until a late hour for the arrival of another priest to be able to participate in the Eucharistic Sacrifice, and be nourished with the food of Heaven.

(15) Furthermore, with the introduction of all kinds of machinery into general use, it very frequently happens that not a few workmen employed in factories or in transportation and seaport jobs, or in other public utility services, are occupied not only in the daytime, but also at night on alternately repeated work shifts, so that their exhausted condition sometimes compels them to take some nourishment, with the result that they are prevented from approaching the Eucharistic table fasting.

16) Mothers of families, likewise, are also frequently unable to go to Holy Communion until they have taken care of their household tasks, which often demand of them many hours of work.

(17) Again it happens that in schools and academies for boys and girls there are a great many who are eager to respond to that divine invitation: " Suffer the little children to come unto Me," because they are utterly confident that He who " feedeth among the lilies " will guard the purity of their souls against the

ipsorum animi candorem morumque integritatem contra iuvenilis aetatis illecebras ac mundi insidias tutetur; verumtamen perdifficile interdum iisdem est, antequam ad scholam se conferant, sacras adire aedes ibique sese Angelico enutrire Pane, postea vero domum redire ut necessarium suscipiant nutrimentum.

(18) Hoc praeterea animadvertendum est saepe hodie contingere ut frequentissimae populi multitudines ex alio ad alium locum postmeridianis horis ea de causa transgrediantur, ut religiosas celebrationes, vel coetus de re sociali habendos participent; si igitur hisce etiam datis occasionibus liceat Eucharisticum peragere Mysterium, quod divinae gratiae vitalis fons est voluntatesque iubet ad virtutem adipiscendam exardescere, haud dubium est inde vim hauriri posse, qua omnes ad christiane penitus sentiendum operandumque excitentur, et ad legitimis etiam obtemperandum legibus.

(19) Peculiaribus hisce considerationibus haec adicere opportunum videtur, quae ad omnes spectant; quamvis nempe nostris hisce temporibus ars medica ac disciplina illa, quae hygiene dicitur, tantos progressus fecerint, tantumque contulerint ad mortuorum numerum in puerili praesertim aetate minuendum, nihilo secius praesentis vitae condiciones atque ea, quae ex immanibus huius saeculi bellis consecuta sunt incommoda, eiusmodi sunt, ut non parum corporum constitutionem valetudinemque debilitaverint.

(20) Hisce de causis, quo praesertim experrecta in Eucharistiam pietas facilius augeatur, e variis Nationibus Episcopi non pauci, officiosis datis litteris petiere, ut haec ieiunii lex aliquantulum mitigaretur; atque iam haec Apostolica Sedes peculiares hac in re facultates ac venias sacrorum administris ac christifidelibus benigne concessit. Ad quas concessiones quod attinet, memorare libet Decretum, quod *Post Editum* inscribitur, a S. Congregatione Concilii die VII mensis Decembris, anno MCMVI, pro infirmis datum;[23] ac Litteras die XXII mensis Maii, anno MCMXXIII, Locorum Ordinariis a S.S.C.S. Officii pro sacerdotibus datas.[24]

[23] *Acta S. Sedis,* XXXIX, 603 sq.

[24] S. S. Congr. S. Officii Litterae Locorum Ordinariis datae super ieiunio eucharistico ante Missam: *Acta Ap. Sedis,* XV, 151 sq.

temptations of youth, and protect the innocence of their lives from the snares of the world. But it is sometimes extremely difficult for them, before they betake themselves to school, to go to the church, there to eat the Bread of Angels, and afterward return home to take the nourishment they need.

(18) Besides, one should notice that frequently nowadays it happens that very large crowds of people move from place to place in the evening hours in order to take part in religious festivities or to hold meetings on social questions. Now if it were allowed on such occasions to celebrate the Eucharistic Mystery, living font of divine grace, which impels the will to burn with the desire of acquiring virtue, there is no doubt that all could draw the strength and inspiration from this source to think and to act in a thoroughly Christian manner, and to give obedience to just laws.

(19) To these specialized considerations it seems appropriate to add some things which concern everyone. Although in our day medical science and the study called hygiene have made great steps forward and have contributed so much to lessening the death rate especially among the young, nevertheless the conditions of modern life and the hardships consequent upon the frightful wars of this century are such as to impair in no small degree bodily health and constitution.

(20) For these reasons, and especially to increase more easily the newly awakened devotion to the Eucharist, many Bishops from various countries have respectfully requested by letter that this law of fasting be somewhat mitigated; and the Apostolic See has already graciously granted special faculties and permissions in this regard to priests and faithful. With regard to these concessions one may recall the decree entitled *Post editum,* issued by the Sacred Congregation of the Council, December 7, 1906, for the sick; and the Letter of May 22, 1923, given to the Ordinaries of places by the Supreme Sacred Congregation of the Holy Office, for the priests.

(21) Postremis hisce temporibus, Episcoporum hac de re petitiones crebriores impensioresque fuere, atque ampliores pariter fuerunt facultates concessae, eae potissimum quae belli occasione dilargitae sunt. Id procul dubio luculenter indicat novas, graves, non intermissas ac satis generales exstare causas, quibus nimis difficile sit, multiplicibus in rerum adiunctis, cum sacerdotes Eucharisticum sacrificium celebrare, tum christifideles Angelico vesci Pane ieiunos.

(22) Quamobrem, ut gravibus hisce incommodis ac difficultatibus occurramus, utque indultorum diversitas in actionum discrepantiam ne cedat, necessarium ducimus Eucharistici ieiunii disciplinam ita mitigando statuere, ut, quam largissime fieri potest, in peculiaribus etiam temporum locorum ac christifidelium condicionibus, eiusmodi legi omnes obtemperare facilius queant. Haec Nos decernentes, fore confidimus ut haud parum conferre possimus ad Eucharisticae pietatis incrementum, atque adeo aptius permovere atque excitare omnes ad Angelorum participandam Mensam, adaucta procul dubio Dei gloria ac Mystici Iesu Christi Corporis sanctimonia.

(23) Haec igitur omnia, quae sequuntur, Apostolica auctoritate Nostra decernimus ac statuimus:

(24) I. Ieiunii eucharistici lex, a media nocte pro iis omnibus vigere pergit, qui in peculiaribus condicionibus non versentur, quas per Apostolicas has Litteras expositurі sumus. Principium tamen generale et commune omnibus in posterum esto, sive sacerdotibus, sive christifidelibus: aquam videlicet naturalem Eucharisticum ieiunium non frangere.

(25) II. Infirmi, etiamsi non decumbant, aliquid sumere possunt, de prudenti confessarii consilio, per modum potus, vel verae medicinae, exceptis alcoholicis. Eadem facultas sacerdotibus infirmis conceditur Missam celebraturis.

(26) III. Sacerdotes, qui vel tardioribus horis, vel post gravem sacri ministerii laborem, vel post longum iter celebraturi sunt, aliquid sumere possunt per modum potus, exclusis alcoholicis; a quo tamen se abstineant saltem per spatium unius horae, ante quam sacris operentur.

(21) During these latter days the petitions of the Bishops in this matter have been more frequent and more insistent, and the faculties granted have been correspondingly more liberal, especially those bestowed by reason of the war. This certainly indicates clearly that there exist new, serious, continuing, and rather general causes which make it too difficult in many circumstances both for priests to celebrate the Eucharistic Sacrifice, and for the faithful to eat the Bread of Angels, fasting.

(22) Wherefore, in order to meet these serious inconveniences and difficulties, and lest the diversity of indults lead to inconsistency in practice, We judge it necessary to establish the discipline of the Eucharistic fast, mitigating it in such a way that as widely as possible, even in the special circumstances of time, of place, and of the faithful, all may be able to observe that law more easily. In issuing this decree, We trust that We will be able to contribute much to the increase of the Eucharistic piety, and so more effectively move and inspire all to participate at the Table of the Angels, to the certain increase of the glory of God, and of the holiness of the Mystical Body of Jesus Christ.

(23) Accordingly, by Our Apostolic Authority We decree and command all the following:

(24) I. The law of the Eucharistic fast from midnight continues in effect for all those who are not in the special circumstances which We are about to explain by these Apostolic Letters. But in the future this shall be a general principle common to all, whether priests or faithful; namely, natural water does not break the Eucharistic fast.

(25) II. The sick, even though not confined to bed, with the prudent advice of a confessor, can take something by way of drink, or of true medicine, excepting alcoholic beverages. The same faculty is granted to sick priests who are going to say Mass.

(26) III. Priests who are going to celebrate either at a rather late hour, or after onerous work of the sacred ministry, or after a long journey, may take something by way of drink, exclusive of alcoholic beverages; they must abstain, however, from such drink at least for the space of one hour before they say Mass.

(27) IV. Qui autem bis, vel ter Missam celebrent, ablutiones sumere possunt, quae tamen, in hoc casu, non vino, sed aqua tantum fieri debent.

(28) V. Christifideles pariter, etiamsi non infirmi, qui ob grave incommodum—hoc est, ob debilitantem laborem, ob tardiores horas, quibus tantum ad Sacram Synaxim accedere possint, vel ob longinquum iter, quod suscipere debeant—ad Eucharisticam mensam omnino ieiuni adire nequeant, de prudenti confessarii consilio, hac perdurante necessitate, aliquid sumere possunt per modum potus, exclusis alcoholicis; a quo tamen se abstineant saltem per spatium unius horae, antequam Angelico enutriantur Pane.

(29) VI. Si rerum adiuncta id necessario postulant, locorum Ordinariis concedimus ut Missae celebrationem vespertinis, ut diximus, horis permittere queant, ita tamen ut haec initium non habeat ante horam IV post meridiem, sive in festis de praecepto, quae adhuc vigent, sive in illis quae olim viguerunt, sive primis uniuscuiusque mensis feriis sextis, sive denique in illis sollemnibus, quae cum magno populi concursu celebrentur, atque etiam, praeter hos dies, semel in hebdomada, servato a sacerdote ieiunio trium horarum quoad cibum solidum et potus alcoholicos, unius autem horae quoad ceteros potus non alcoholicos. In his autem Missis christifideles ad Sacram Synaxim accedere poterunt, hac eadem servata norma ad ieiunium Eucharisticum quod attinet, firmo praescripto can. 857.

(30) Evangelii autem praeconibus, in territoriis Missionum, peculiarissimis perpensis condicionibus in quibus versantur, ob quas raro plerumque habentur sacerdotes, qui longinquas stationes invisere queant, Locorum Ordinarii eiusmodi facultates concedere poterunt ceteris etiam hebdomadis diebus.

(31) Locorum tamen Ordinarii diligenter curent, ut quaelibet vitetur interpretatio, quae concessas facultates amplificet, utque ab omni abusu et irreverentia hac in re caveatur; in hisce enim dilargiendis facultatibus, quas hominum, locorum temporumque condiciones hodie postulant, Nos etiam atque etiam volumus Eucharistici ieiunii momentum, vim atque efficacitatem confirmare ad eos quod attinet, qui Divinum Redemptorem sub Eucharisticis velis latentem accepturi sunt. Ac praeterea, quotiescumque cor-

(27) IV. Those who say Mass twice or three times may take the ablutions; in this case, however, the ablutions should be done not with wine, but only with water.

(28) V. The faithful in like manner, even though not sick, who, because of a grave inconvenience—that is, because of exhausting labor, or because they can draw near the Holy Banquet only at a rather late hour, or because of a long journey which they must make—cannot approach the Eucharistic table completely fasting, may with the prudent advice of a confessor, as long as the need lasts, take something by way of drink, exclusive of alcoholic beverages; they must abstain, however, from such drink at least for the space of one hour before they are nourished by the Bread of Angels.

(29) VI. If the circumstances necessarily require it, We grant to the Ordinaries of places the faculty of permitting the celebration of Mass during the evening hours, as We said, but in such wise that Mass shall not begin before four o'clock in the afternoon: on holy days of obligation still in force, on those formerly in force, on the First Friday of each month, and on those solemnities which are celebrated with a great concourse of people, and also in addition to these days, once each week, provided the priest observes a fast of three hours from solid food and alcoholic beverages, and one hour from other, non-alcoholic beverages. At these Masses the faithful may approach the Sacred Banquet, observing the same norm with regard to the Eucharistic fast, the prescription of can. 857 remaining in force.

(30) In Mission territories, the Ordinaries of places can grant the same faculties on the other days of the week also to the heralds of the Gospel, in view of the very unusual conditions in which they find themselves, because of which, generally speaking, there rarely are priests who can visit the distant stations.

(31) But let Ordinaries of places carefully see to it that any interpretation which would amplify the faculties granted be avoided, and that all abuse and irreverence in this matter be guarded against; for in bestowing these faculties, required today by the conditions of men, of places, and of the times, We wish to confirm again and again the importance, the force, and the efficacy of the Eucharistic fast for those who are going to receive our Divine Redeemer hidden under Eucharistic veils. And be-

poris incommodum minuitur, animus debet pro facultate rem supplere, sive interna paenitentia, sive aliis modis, ex tradito Ecclesiae more; quae quidem cum ieiunium mitigat, alia opera adimplenda imperare solet. Qui igitur datis hac in re facultatibus perfrui queant, impensiores ad Caelum admoveant preces, quibus Deum adorent, eidem grates agant, ac praesertim admissa expient novaque impetrent superna auxilia. Cum omnes perspectum habeant oporteat Eucharistiam " tamquam passionis suae memoriale perenne " [25] a Iesu Christo institutam fuisse, ex animis sensus illos eliciant christianae humilitatis christianaeque paenitentiae, quos Divini Redemptoris cruciatuum ac mortis meditatio excitare debet. Itemque eidem Divino Redemptori, qui perpetuo in altaribus se immolans, maximum renovat sui amoris documentum, adauctos offerant omnes suae erga proximos caritatis fructus. Hac profecto ratione conferent omnes ad illud Apostoli gentium cotidie magis explendum: " Unus panis, unum corpus multi sumus, omnes qui de uno pane participamus ".[26]

(32) Quaecumque autem hisce Litteris decreta continentur, ea omnia stabilia, rata ac valida esse volumus, contrariis, quibuslibet non obstantibus, peculiarissima etiam mentione dignis; atque abolitis ceteris omnibus privilegiis ac facultatibus, quomodocumque a Sancta Sede concessis, ut ubique omnes hanc disciplinam aeque riteque servent.

(33) Quae quidem omnia, supra statuta, vim suam obtineant a promulgationis die per *Acta Apostolicae Sedis* factae.

(34) Datum Romae, apud S. Petrum, anno Domini millesimo nongentesimo quinquagesimo tertio, die sexta mensis Ianuarii, in Epiphania Domini, Pontificatus Nostri anno quarto decimo.[27]

PIUS PP. XII.

[25] S. Thom., *Opusc.* LVII, Offic. de Festo Corporis Christi, lect. IV. *Opera omnia,* Romae, MDLXX, Vol. XVII.

[26] *I Cor.,* X, 17.

[27] The above numeration is that devised by the Reverend John C. Ford. S.J., in his work entitled " The New Eucharistic Legislation "

sides, whenever the discomfort of the body is lessened, the soul should, as far as it can, supply for it, either by interior penance, or by some other means in accord with the traditional custom of the Church; which is wont to command other works to be done when it mitigates the fast. Hence those who can make use of the faculties granted in this matter should raise more fervent prayers to Heaven, to adore God, to offer Him thanks, and most of all to expiate their deeds and to gain new help from on high. Since all should recognize that the Eucharist has been instituted by Jesus Christ "as the perennial memorial of His passion," let them elicit from their hearts those sentiments of Christian humility and Christian penance which meditation on the sufferings and death of our Divine Redeemer should arouse. Likewise let all offer to our Divine Redeemer, who ever immolating Himself on our altars renews the greatest proof of His love, increased fruits of charity toward their neighbors. In this way, certainly, all will contribute daily to the greater fulfillment of that saying of the Apostle of the Gentiles: "For we, being many, are one bread, one body, all that partake of one bread."

(32) Whatever decrees are contained in these Letters We wish to be established, ratified, and valid, notwithstanding any dispositions to the contrary, even those worthy of most special mention; and since all other privileges and faculties, no matter how granted by the Holy See, are abolished, We desire that everyone everywhere give due and proper observance to the new discipline.

(33) Let all that has been decreed above take effect from the day of its promulgation made by means of the *Acta Apostolicae Sedis*.

(34) Given at St. Peter's in Rome, in the year of Our Lord one thousand nine hundred and fifty-three, on the sixth day of the month of January, on the Epiphany of Our Lord, in the fourteenth year of Our Pontificate.

POPE PIUS XII.

SUPREMA SACRA CONGREGATIO S. OFFICII
INSTRUCTIO

De Disciplina Circa Ieiunium Eucharisticum Servanda

Constitutio Apostolica *Christus Dominus,* hoc ipso die a Summo Pontifice Pio XII, feliciter regnante, data, largitur quidem non paucas facultates ac dispensationes circa legis ieiunii eucharistici observantiam, sed normas maxima ex parte quoad substantiam quoque confirmat Codicis Iuris Canonici (can. 808 et 858, 1) impositas sacerdotibus et fidelibus, qui eidem legi obtemperare queant. Attamen hisce etiam extenditur favorabile ipsius Constitutionis primum praescriptum, cuius vi aqua *naturalis* (id est sine ulla cuiuslibet elementi adiectione) non amplius frangit ieiunium eucharisticum (Const., n. I). Quod vero attinet ad ceteras concessiones, iis tantum uti possunt sacerdotes et fideles, qui in peculiaribus versantur condicionibus, de quibus in Constitutione cautum est, vel Missas vespertinas celebrant aut in iisdem sacram communionem recipiunt ex licentia Ordinariorum, intra limites novarum facultatum, quae iisdem tributae sunt.

Itaque, ut normae ad huiusmodi concessiones pertinentes ubique conformi ratione serventur atque evitetur quaelibet interpretatio, quae concessas facultates amplificet, utque ab omni abusu hac de re caveatur, Suprema haec Sacra Congregatio Sancti Officii, iussu mandatuque Summi ipsius Pontificis, statuit quae sequuntur:

Quoad infirmos sive fideles sive sacerdotes
(Const., n. II)

1. Fideles infirmi, etiamsi non decumbant, aliquid sumere possunt per modum potus, exceptis alcoholicis, si, suae infirmitatis causa, usque ad sacrae communionis receptionem ieiunium, absque gravi incommodo, nequeunt servare integrum; possunt etiam aliquid sumere per modum medicinae, sive liquidum (exclusis alcoholicis), sive solidum, dummodo de vera medicina agatur, a medico praescripta vel uti tali vulgo recepta. Adverten-

THE SUPREME SACRED CONGREGATION OF THE HOLY OFFICE INSTRUCTION

On the Discipline to be Observed Concerning the Eucharistic Fast

The Apostolic Constiturion *Christus Dominus,* issued this very day by the Sovereign Pontiff Pius XII, happily reigning, grants not a few faculties and dispensations with regard to the observance of the law of the Eucharistic fast, but also confirms for the most part in their substance the norms of the Code of Canon Law (can. 808 and 858, § 1) binding on priests and faithful who are able to observe those norms. Nevertheless, to these also is extended the favorable first prescription of the Constitution itself, in virtue of which *natural* water (that is, without the addition of any element whatsoever) no longer breaks the Eucharistic fast (Const., n. I). But as regards the other concessions, they can be used only by priests and by the faithful who are in the special conditions provided for in the Constitution, or who say evening Masses or receive Communion at such Masses with the permission of the Ordinaries, within the limits of the new faculties which have been granted to them.

And so, in order that the norms relative to such concessions may be everywhere uniformly observed and to avoid any interpretation which would amplify the faculties granted, and in order to provide against every abuse in this matter, this Supreme Sacred Congregation of the Holy Office, at the direction and by the command of the Sovereign Pontiff himself, decrees as follows:

Concerning the sick, both faithful and priests (Const., n. II)

1. The faithful who are sick, even though not confined to bed, can take something by way of drink, except alcoholic drinks, if, by reason of their sickness, they are unable to observe the complete fast until the reception of Holy Communion without grave inconvenience; they can also take something by way of true medicine, either liquid (exclusive of alcohol), or solid, as long as

dum autem est, non posse tamquam medicina haberi quodlibet solidum pro nutrimento sumptum.

2. Condiciones, quibus quis dispensatione a lege ieiunii frui possit, nulla adiecta ante communionem temporis limitatione, prudenter a confessario perpendendae sunt, neque quisquam sine eius consilio uti potest. Confessarius autem suum consilium dare poterit sive in foro interno sacramentali, sive in foro interno extra-sacramentali, etiam semel pro semper, perdurantibus eiusdem infirmitatis condicionibus.

3. Sacerdotes infirmi, etiamsi non decumbant, dispensatione pariter uti possunt, sive sint Missam celebraturi, sive sanctissimam Eucharistiam recepturi.

Quoad sacerdotes qui in peculiaribus adiunctis versantur
(Const., nn. III et IV)

4. Sacerdotes non infirmi, qui a) vel *tardioribus horis* (i.e. post horam nonam), b) vel *post gravem sacri ministerii laborem* (v. gr. iam a summo mane seu per longum tempus), c) vel *post longum iter* (i.e. saltem 2 km. circiter pedibus percurrendum, vel proportionate longius pro variis vehiculis adhibitis, difficultatis quoque itineris vel personae habita ratione), celebraturi sunt, aliquid sumere possunt per modum potus, exclusis alcoholicis.

5. Tres casus supra numerati tales sunt, ut omnia comprehendant rerum adiuncta, in quibus legislator praefatam facultatem concedere intendit ideoque quaelibet vitetur interpretatio quae facultates concessas amplificet.

6. Sacerdotes, qui in hisce adiunctis versantur aliquid sumere possunt per modum potus semel vel pluries, servato ieiunio unius horae ante Missae celebrationem.

7. Praeterea omnes sacerdotes, qui bis vel ter sunt Missam celebraturi, possunt in prioribus Missis duas ablutiones a rubricis Missalis praescriptas sumere, sed tantum adhibita aqua, quae quidem, iuxta novum principium, ieiunium non frangit.

Qui tamen die Nativitatis Domini vel in Commemoratione omnium fidelium defunctorum tres Missas sine intermissione celebrat, quod ad ablutiones attinet, rubricas observare tenetur.

there is question of true medicine, prescribed by a physician, or commonly accepted as such. It is to be noted, however, that not every solid taken as nourishment can be considered medicine.

2. The conditions under which one can enjoy the dispensation from the law of fasting, with no time limit prescribed before Communion, must be prudently weighed by a confessor, nor can anyone use the dispensation without his advice. A confessor, however, can give his advice either in the sacramental internal forum, or in the extra-sacramental internal forum. He can also give it once and for all as long as the conditions of the same sickness last.

3. Sick priests, even though not confined to bed, can use the dispensation in like manner, whether they are going to say Mass, or receive the most Holy Eucharist.

Concerning priests who are in special circumstances
(Const., nn. III and IV)

4. Priests who are not sick, who are going to celebrate a) either *at a rather late hour* (i.e., after nine o'clock), b) or *after onerous work of the sacred ministry* (for example, from early morning or for a long time), c) or *after a long journey* (i.e., at least about two kilometers to be traversed on foot, or proportionately longer according to the type of vehicle used, taking into consideration also the difficulty of the journey or of the person), can take something by way of drink, exclusive of alcoholic beverages.

5. The three cases above-mentioned are such as to include all the circumstances in which the legislator intends to grant the aforesaid faculty, and accordingly any interpretation is to be avoided which would amplify the faculties granted.

6. Priests who are in these circumstances can take something by way of drink once or several times, if they observe one hour's fast before the celebration of Mass.

7. Furthermore, all priests who are going to say Mass twice or three times, may, in the prior Masses, take the two ablutions prescribed by the rubrics of the Missal, but using only water, which, of course, according to the new principle, does not break the fast. But one who celebrates three Masses one after the other on Christmas Day or on All Souls' Day is obliged to observe the rubrics with regard to the ablutions.

8. Si vero sacerdos, qui bis vel ter Missam celebrare debet, per inadvertentiam vinum quoque in ablutione sumat, non vetatur quominus secundam et tertiam Missam celebret.

Quoad fideles qui in peculiaribus adiunctis versantur
(Const., n. V)

9. Fidelibus pariter, qui non infirmitatis causa, sed *ob aliud grave incommodum* ieiunium eucharisticum servare nequeunt, aliquid sumere licet per modum potus, exceptis tamen alcoholicis et servato ieiunio unius horae ante sacrae communionis receptionem.

10. Causae autem *gravis incommodi* tres enumerantur, quas extendere non licet.

a) *Labor debilitans* ante sacram communionem susceptus.

Hoc labore afficiuntur tum opifices, qui, officinis vel vehicularibus maritimisque muneribus vel aliis publicae utilitatis officiis addicti, diu noctuque per vices occupantur; tum illi, qui ex officio vel ex caritate noctem vigilem transigunt (v. gr. valetudinarii, custodes nocturni, etc.); tum mulieres praegnantes et matresfamilias quae, antequam ecclesiam adire queant, in domesticis negotiis per longum tempus incumbere debent; etc.

b) *Hora tardior, qua sacra communio recipitur.*

Sunt enim haud pauci fideles, qui tantummodo serioribus horis possunt apud se sacerdotem habere, qui sacris operetur; sunt pueri complures, quibus nimis grave est, antequam ad scholam se conferant, ecclesiam adire, angelico pane vesci, postea vero domum reverti, ientaculi sumendi gratia; etc.

c) *Longum iter peragendum,* ut ad ecclesiam perveniatur.

Longum autem hac super re habendum iter, ut supra explicatum est (n. 4), si saltem 2 km. circiter pedibus percurrendum, vel proportionate longius pro variis vehiculis adhibitis, difficultatis quoque itineris vel personae habita ratione.

11. Causae quidem gravis incommodi sunt prudenter a confessario pensitandae in foro interno sacramentali vel non sacramentali; neque absque eiusdem consilio fideles non ieiuni sanctis-

8. But if a priest who has to celebrate Mass twice or three times should inadvertently take wine also in the ablution, he is not forbidden to say the second and third Mass.

Concerning the faithful who are in special circumstances
(Const., n. V)

9. The faithful in like manner who are unable to observe the Eucharistic fast, not by reason of sickness but *because of some other grave inconvenience,* are allowed to take something by way of drink, except, however, alcoholic beverages, and provided they observe one hour's fast before the reception of Holy Communion.

10. The causes of *the grave inconvenience* number three, and it is not permitted to extend them.

a) *Exhausting labor* undertaken before Holy Communion.

Subject to such labor are, first, workmen who are employed on day and night shifts in factories, or in transportation and seaport jobs, or in other public utility services; then those who by reason of their office or by reason of charity stay up during the night (for example, nurses, night watchmen, etc.); then, pregnant women and mothers of families who, before they can go to church, must engage in household tasks for a long time; etc.

b) *The rather late hour when Holy Communion is received.*

For there are not a few of the faithful who only at a rather late hour have a priest in their midst to say Mass; there are a great many children for whom it is too difficult, before they betake themselves to school, to go to church, eat of the Bread of Angels, and then afterward return home to take breakfast; etc.

c) *A long journey to be traveled* to reach the Church.

However, as was explained above (n. 4), a journey is to be considered long in this matter, if at least about two kilometers must be traversed on foot, or a proportionately longer journey according to the type of vehicle used, taking into consideration also the difficulty of the journey or of the person.

11. The causes of the grave inconvenience are to be prudently pondered by a confessor in the sacramental or non-sacramental internal forum; nor can the faithful who are not fasting receive

simam Eucharistiam recipere possunt. Confessarius autem consilium eiusmodi dare potest etiam *semel pro semper*, causa eadem gravis incommodi perdurante.

Quoad Missas vespertinas
(Const., n. VI)

Constitutionis vi *Ordinarii locorum* (cfr. can. 198) facultate fruuntur permittendi in proprio territorio Missae vespertinae celebrationem, si adiuncta id necessario exigunt, praescripto can. 821, § 1, non obstante. Bonum enim commune aliquando sacrorum mysteriorum celebrationem post meridiem expostulat; v. gr. pro quarundam industriarum opificibus, qui festis quoque diebus laboribus succedunt in vices; pro illis operariorum classibus, qui matutinis festorum horis occupantur, ut muneribus portuum addicti; pro iis pariter, qui ex dissitis etiam regionibus maxima frequentia in unum locum conveniunt, ad quandam festivitatem religiosam vel socialem celebrandam, etc.

12. Tamen eiusmodi Missae celebrari possunt non ante horam quartam post meridiem, ac tantummodo in certis diebus *taxative* statutis, seu.

a) festis de praecepto vigentibus, ad normam can. 1247, § 1;

b) festis de praecepto suppressis, iuxta Indicem a. S. Congregatione Concilii editum, die 28 Decembris 1919 (cfr. *A.A.S.*, vol. XII (1920), pp. 42-43);

c) primis cuiusque mensis feriis sextis;

d) ceteris sollemnibus, qui cum magno populi concursu celebrantur;

e) die uno in hebdomada, praeter dies supra memoratos, si bonum peculiarum personarum classium id postulat.

13. Sacerdotes, qui pomeridianis horis Missam celebrant, itemque fideles qui in eadem sacram communionem recipiunt, possunt *inter refectionem,* permissam usque ad tres horas ante Missae vel communionis initium, sumere *congrua moderatione* alcoholicas quoque potiones inter mensam suetas (v. gr. vinum, cerevisiam,

the most Holy Eucharist without his advice. A confessor, however, can also give such advice once and for all, as long as the same cause of grave inconvenience lasts.

Concerning evening Masses.
(Const., n. VI)

By virtue of the Constitution *Ordinaries of Places* (Cf. can. 198) enjoy the faculty of permitting the celebration of evening Mass in their own territory, if the circumstances necessarily require it, notwithstanding the prescription of can. 821, § 1. For the common good sometimes demands the celebration of the sacred mysteries after midday: for example, for workmen in certain industries, who work their shifts even on feast days; for those categories of workers who are employed on feast-day mornings, for example, those employed in seaport jobs; for those who have come from distant regions and gathered together in very large numbers for the celebration of some religious or social festivity.

12. However, such Masses may not be celebrated before four o'clock in the afternoon, and only on certain days, *taxatively* established, to wit:

(a) On existing holy days of obligation, in accordance with can. 1247, § 1;

(b) On suppressed holy days of obligation, according to the Index published by the Sacred Congregation of the Council, December 28, 1919 (cf. *A.A.S.* vol. XII (1920), pp. 42-43);

(c) On the First Friday of each month;

(d) On other solemnities which are celebrated with a great concourse of people;

(e) On one day each week in addition to the above mentioned days, if the good of special classes of persons demands it.

13. Priests who say Mass in the afternoon, as well as the faithful who receive communion at such a Mass, may *during the meal,* permitted up to three hours before the beginning of Mass or Communion, also take, *with appropriate moderation,* the alcoholic beverages customary at table (for example, wine, beer, etc.), liquors being excluded. With regard to the beverages which they

etc.), exclusis quidem liquoribus. Quoad potus autem, quos sumere possunt ante vel post dictam refectionem, usque ad unam horam ante Missam vel communionem, excluditur *omne alcoholicorum genus.*

14. Sacerdotes, eodem die, nequeunt mane et vespere Sacrum litare, nisi potestatem expressam bis terve Missam celebrandi habeant, ad normam can. 806.

Fideles pariter, eodem die, nequeunt mane et vespere ad sacram Synaxim accedere, ad praescriptum can. 857.

15. Fideles, quamvis non sint de eorum numero, pro quibus Missa vespertina forte instituta sit, ad sacram Synaxim libere accedere possunt, *infra dictam Missam vel proxime ante et statim post* (cfr. can. 846, 1), servatis, quod attinet ad ieiunium eucharisticum, normis supra relatis.

16. In locis vero, ubi non *ius commune,* sed *ius missionum* viget, Ordinarii Missas vespertinas omnibus in hebdomada diebus, iisdem condicionibus, permittere possunt.

Monita ad normas exsequendas

17. Ordinarii sedulo invigilent, ut omnis abusus et irreverentia erga sanctissimum Sacramentum plane vitetur.

18. Pariter curent, ut nova disciplina a cunctis subditis uniformiter observentur, eosque doceant, omnes facultates et dispensationes, tum territoriales tum personales, hactenus a Sancta Sede concessas, abrogatas esse.

19. Constitutionis atque huius Instructionis interpretatio textui fideliter adhaereat, neque ullo modo facultates tam favorabiles amplificet. Quod ad consuetudines attinet, quibus a nova disciplina discrepare contingat, clausula illa abrogativa animadvertenda est: " contrariis quibuslibet non obstantibus, peculiarissima etiam mentione dignis."

20. Ordinarii et sacerdotes, qui datis a Sancta Sede facultatibus perfrui debent, fideles studiose excitent, ut frequenter Missae Sacrificio adstare velint et pane eucharistico reficiantur opportunisque inceptis, praesertim sacra praedicatione, illud promove-

may take before or after the aforesaid meal, up to one hour before Mass or Communion, *all kinds of alcoholic beverages* are excluded.

14. Priests may not say Mass morning and evening the same day, unless they have the express faculty of celebrating Mass twice or three times, in accordance with can. 806.

Likewise the faithful may not the same day approach the Holy Table morning and evening, according to the prescription of Can. 857.

15. The faithful, even if they are not of the number of those for whom the evening Mass may have been granted, can freely approach the Holy Table *during the aforesaid Mass,* or *just before and just after* (cf. can. 846, 1), if they have observed the norms set down above concerning the Eucharistic fast.

16. In places where not the general law but the law of the missions is in force. Ordinaries can permit evening Masses on all the days of the week, under the same conditions.

Directions for putting the norms into effect

17. Ordinaries must carefully see to it that every abuse and irreverence toward the Most Blessed Sacrament is entirely avoided.

18. They must likewise take care that the new discipline be uniformly observed by all their subjects, and they must instruct them that all faculties and dispensations, whether territorial or personal, heretofore granted by the Holy See, are abrogated.

19. The interpretation of the Constitution and of this Instruction must faithfully keep to the text, and must not in any way enlarge the highly favorable faculties which have been granted. With regard to customs which may differ from the new discipline, let the abrogating clause be kept in mind: "Notwithstanding any disposition whatever to the contrary, even those worthy of most special mention."

20. Let Ordinaries and priests, who are going to use the faculties granted by the Holy See, zealously exhort the faithful to assist frequently at the sacrifice of the Mass and be refreshed by the bread of the Eucharist, and let them promote by opportune measures, especially by preaching, that spiritual good in view of

ant spirituale bonum, cuius adipiscendi gratia Summus Pontifex Pius XII Constitutionem edere voluit.

Summus Pontifex, hanc Instructionem approbans, statuit ut ipsa promulgetur per editionem in *Actis Apostolicae Sedis* una cum Constitutione Apostolica *Christus Dominus.*

Ex Aedibus Sancti Officii, die VI mensis Ianuarii, anno MDCCCCLIII.

I. Card. PIZZARDO, *a Secretis*

L. S. A. Ottaviani, *Adsessor*

which the Sovereign Pontiff Pius XII has been pleased to publish the Constitution.

The Sovereign Pontiff, approving this Instruction, decreed that it should be promulgated by publication in *Acta Apostolicae Sedis,* together with the Apostolic Constitution *Christus Dominus.*

From the palace of the Holy Office, on the 6th day of January, in the year 1953.

J. Card. PIZZARDO, *Secretary*

L. S. A. Ottaviani, *Assesor*

PART II
CANONICAL COMMENTARY

CHAPTER I
PRELIMINARY NOTIONS

Article 1. Historical Background

The Church, the guardian and dispenser of the sacraments, has from the beginning been singularly solicitous in taking all precautions against the profanation of any of them. This is especially true of the sacrament of the Most Holy Eucharist. The Church has, for this reason, from earliest times prescribed that those who receive it should observe the natural fast from the previous midnight. It was not until the end of the thirteenth century, however, that the nature of the Eucharistic fast was clearly defined. The principles governing it were formulated by St. Thomas (1225–1274) at that time. He clearly distinguished the ecclesiastical fast from the natural or Eucharistic fast, which consisted in abstaining from all food and drink of whatever nature, even from anything taken as medicine from the previous midnight. While the former admitted of slightness of matter the latter did not.[1]

While it is certain the the law of the Eucharistic fast dates back to the second century, if not also to Apostolic times, it is equally certain that it is a law of purely ecclesiastical origin. One knows this from the fact that Christ and the Apostles were not fasting at the Last Supper. Nor is there any evidence to indicate that Christ gave a positive precept to His Apostles after the Last Supper. There is positive proof, however, that the law was in existence at the beginning of the third century. The *Apostolic Tradition* of St. Hippolytus of Rome, written sometime between 200–222, states: "Let everyone of the faithful be careful to partake of the Eucharist before he eats any-

[1] St. Thomas, *Summa Theologica* (6 vols., Taurini: Marietti, 1926), Pars III, q. LXXX, a. 8.

thing else."[2] Moreover, fasting was prescribed for priests celebrating Mass by various councils at the end of the fourth century. Thus, in the year 393 the Council of Hippo decreed: "The Sacrament of the Altar must not be celebrated but by those who are fasting."[3]

Like all ecclesiastical laws, the Church can and does dispense from its obligation. The Council of Constance in the year 1415, while reaffirming the ancient law of the fast, added a certain qualification: ". . . the authority of the Sacred Canons, together with the praiseworthy authorized usage of the Church, has maintained and does maintain, that this Sacrament should not be celebrated after supper, nor should it be received by the faithful not fasting, except in a case of sickness, or in a case of other necessity recognized by law or permitted by the Church."[4]

It was not until the beginning of the twentieth century, however, that general dispensations from the strict wording of the law were granted. On December 7, 1906, Pope St. Pius X issued through the Congregation of the Council the Decree *Post editum*, granting a general dispensation that enabled the sick to receive Holy Communion with relative ease and frequency.[5]

The relaxation granted by this decree entitled the sick who had been in bed for a month without reasonable hope of a speedy recovery and who were unable to observe the natural fast to take some liquid food before Communion. It provided that those who were affected by the peculiar circumstances postulated in the law could receive once or twice a month if they lived at home, once or twice a week if they lived in a religious house, hospital or place in which the Blessed Sacrament was reserved, or if they enjoyed the privilege of assisting at Mass in a pri-

[2] *The Treatise on the Apostolic Tradition of St. Hippolytus of Rome*, edited by Rev. Gregory Dix, O.S.B. (London: MacMillan, 1937), p. 58.

[3] Can. 28—Joannes D. Mansi, *Sacrorum Conciliorum Nova et Amplissima Collectio* (53 vols. in 60, Parisiis, Arnhemii, Lipsiae, 1901-1927), III, 923 (hereafter cited as Mansi).

[4] Sess. XIII—Mansi, XXVII, 727.

[5] S.C.C., 7 dec. 1906—*Codicis Iuris Canonici Fontes*, cura Emī Petri Card. Gasparri editi (9 vols., Romae postea, Civitate Vaticana: Typis Polyglottis Vaticanis, 1923-1939; Vols VII-IX, ed. cura Emī Iustiniani Card. Serédi), n. 433 (hereafter cited *Fontes*).

vate oratory. Under no circumstance, however, could they without fasting receive Communion daily.

This concession was later incorporated into the universal law of the Church. Canon 858, § 2, stated that the sick who had been confined to bed for a month without reasonable hope of a speedy recovery could with the prudent advice of a confessor receive Holy Communion once or twice each week even though they had taken medicine or liquid food beforehand. Hence, the law of the Code of Canon Law, like the decree of 1906, demanded that all who were not affected by the postulated peculiar circumstances were to observe the natural fast from the previous midnight, and even those who were entitled to use the concession could do so only once or twice each week.

With the promulgation of the Apostolic Constitution *Christus Dominus* on January 6, 1953, and the accompanying Instruction of the Supreme Sacred Congregation of the Holy Office on the same day, the law of the Eucharistic fast was further relaxed.[6]

The motives that prompted these relaxations are enumerated by the Pope in the introductory paragraphs of the Apostolic Constitution. They are five in number. The first is the extraordinary growth in the practise of frequent and daily Communion in modern times. Undoubtedly, many persons who could receive monthly or even weekly without grave inconvenience or without endangering their health might have serious difficulty in observing the natural fast daily. The result was that many people who wished to communicate daily were unable to do so.

The second reason, namely, the changing character of modern society from agricultural and rural life to industrial and urban life weakened the endurance of mankind. For this reason, the citizens of the present-day world are unable to endure the hardships their ancestors regarded as part of everyday life. Consequently, it often happened that persons who wished to approach the Table of the Lord daily were, because of their physical dispositions, deprived of so doing.

[6] Constitutio Apostolica *Christus Dominus,* 6 ian. 1953, De disciplina servanda quoad ieiunium eucharisticum, *Acta Apostolica Sedis* (*AAS*) (Romae, 1909-), XLV (1953), 15-24, and 47-51 (hereafter cited as the Apostolic Constitution and the Instruction respectively).

The third reason mentioned by the Pope was the scarcity of vocations to the priesthood. Thus, the clergy were overtaxed and naturally their health suffered. In consequence there was a smaller number of the clergy to cope with the ever-growing work in the ministry.

Fourthly, many members of the hierarchy from different countries had made and continued to make representations to the Holy Father for individual and local dispensations.

These four reasons plus the fact that the Pope wished to preserve a uniform practice throughout the universal Church urged him to issue the Apostolic Constitution *Christus Dominus.*

Article 2. Nature and Interpretation of the Constitution *Christus Dominus.*

The juridic nature of the new legislation has been the subject of much discussion among canonists since its promulgation. The specific question as to whether the Holy Father intended to formulate a new law for the universal Church or to grant merely certain concessions and dispensations to those who were affected by the peculiar circumstances mentioned in the law has been widely debated. This question is of vital importance, for upon its decision rests the interpretation of the whole law. If, on the one hand, one were to regard it as a new law for the universal Church, then it should be interpreted according to the general norms of interpretation in line with what is enacted in the Code of Canon Law.[7]

On the other hand, if one were to see in it a law containing an exception to the general law of the Eucharistic fast, one would be obliged to interpret it according to the norms of canon 19. A third possibility, namely that it is a dispensation or a relaxation of a law in a particular case, cannot be sustained, for, as Michiels shows, when a dispensation from the obligation of the law is granted to the whole community for which the law was made, such a dispensation, if it is to be classified juridically as such, must be a temporary one.[8] Here, however, the dispensation is not temporary. The fact that water no longer breaks

[7] Can. 18.

[8] Cf. *Normae Generales Iuris Canonici* (2. ed. 2 vols., Parisiis-Tornaci-Romae: Desclée et Socii, 1949), II, 678.

the fast is not a temporary ruling. It is the permanent law for all Catholics. The same may be said for the other concessions. They are not temporary but permanent ones, namely concessions contained in the law itself.

Nor can it be regarded as a privilege, for this word is used only once in the Constitution, and then in reference to previous indults only.[9] Moreover, as Father Reed [10] so succinctly stated, the concessions are not granted as a matter of private convenience or for the good of individuals. While the relaxations do benefit individuals, the primary intention of the legislator was not to make the law easier for the subjects, but by means of making it easier to promote the glory of God and the sanctity of the Church as a whole. This purpose the Holy Father solemnly expressed in the Constitution: " In issuing this decree, We trust that We will be able to contribute much to the increase of Eucharistic piety, and so more effectively move and inspire all to participate at the Table of the Angels, to the certain increase of the glory of God, and of the holiness of the Mystical Body of Jesus Christ." [11]

The question to be decided therefore is: Can the new legislation be regarded as a new law for the universal Church, or merely as a law containing an exception from the general law of Eucharistic fast? In order to resolve this question, two principles of law must be brought to bear upon that matter. The first, as utilized in canon 22, states that a subsequent law abrogates a former law, if it expressly says so, if it is directly contrary to it, or if it entirely revises the whole subject-matter of the former law. The second states that in a case of doubt the revocation of a pre-existing law is not presumed, and hence the subsequent laws should be adapted to the prior laws, and should as far as possible be made to harmonize with them.[12]

Before applying the principle enunciated in canon 22 to the present legislation, one may well note that a law may be revoked either expressly or tacitly. Express revocation is had when the

[9] Cf. Apostolic Constitution, n. 32.

[10] Cf. "Select Questions on the Eucharistic Fast," *Theological Studies*, XVI (1955), 39.

[11] Apostolic Constitution, n. 22.

[12] Cf. canon 23.

legislator revokes the law in manifest terms or inserts abrogatory or derogatory clauses such as: *notwithstanding anything to the contrary* or *notwithstanding in any respect anything to the contrary, though worthy of special mention.*[13] Tacit revocation, on the other hand, is had when a new law is issued directly contrary to the former law, or when a new law takes up and readjusts the entire subject-matter of the former law.

In the law under discussion, while the legislator does not revoke the former law in manifest terms, he does insert the required abrogatory and derogatory clauses in the Constitution itself. In fact, the identical clause quoted above as the one necessary for express revocation is mentioned: "Whatever decrees are contained in these Letters We wish to be established, ratified and valid, *notwithstanding any dispositions to the contrary, even those worthy of most special mention.*"[14] This phrase is here used in its legal juridical sense and it can be interpreted only as an express revocation of the former law.

But even though some might argue that the words here used do not fulfill the requirements of an express revocation, there is still sufficient evidence to show a tacit revocation. Surely it must be admitted that the present law is "directly contrary" to the former one. Whereas the former law forbade the use of any food, drink, or medicine from the previous midnight, the present legislation decrees as a general principle that water no longer breaks the Eucharistic fast. This is a perfect example of tacit revocation, for when two laws cannot stand either wholly or partially, that is, when the new law on one and the same matter decrees something different from the old law, it is understood that the later law abrogates the former law or derogates from it. In the present case the contrariety is so evident that the laws are incompatible.

Again, it is useless to appeal to the introductory part of the Instruction, wherein it is mentioned that the norms of canons 808 and 858, § 1, are confirmed for the most part in the new law. This is no proof that the former law is not abrogated. Rather,

[13] Cf. Van Hove, *De Legibus Ecclesiasticis* (Mechliniae-Romae: Dessain, 1930), p. 352.

[14] Cf. Apostolic Constitution, n. 32.

the implication is that the law as stated in these canons has been revoked, but that the new law replacing it is very similar at least in substance, e.g., the law of the Eucharistic fast (water excepted) still begins at midnight. Nor does it avail one to refer to the very first norm of the Constitution, where it is stated that "the law of the Eucharistic fast from midnight continues in effect for all those who are not in the special circumstances which We are about to explain by these Apostolic Letters," as an indication that the former law is not totally repealed. The very next sentence in that same law decrees that water no longer breaks the fast, which is a complete change from the former law.

Furthermore, it is futile to contend that the new legislation is not a total reconstruction of the Code law, inasmuch as the rules for the reception of Viaticum and for the prevention of irreverence remain unchanged. Those who use this argument should remember that for a total reorganization of the subject-matter it is not necessary that everything contained in the new law reflect a total change from the former one. As Van Hove (1872–1947) stated, the fact that the dispositions of a former law are incorporated in the new one is an indication of the total reorganization of the former one.[15]

Many canonists are reluctant to admit that the precept of canon 858, § 2, is repealed. The alleged reason for their reluctance is that the sick are seemingly in a worse position than they were under the Code law, though the present legislation purports to mitigate the rigors of the former law. It is true that the sick under the former law were entitled to take liquids, including alcoholic ones, before the reception of Holy Communion, whereas in the present dispensation alcoholic beverages are completely prohibited. However, anomalies of this kind are found in practically every law, but this of itself is not a sufficient reason for concluding that the law in question has not been repealed. If one were to follow this line of reasoning one would be compelled to adopt the strange position of retaining that portion of the law which was favorable and of rejecting the less favorable part.

[15] Cf. *De Legibus Ecclesiasticis,* p. 355.

Secondly, to state that the former law was more favorable for the sick is debatable. While the former law allowed liquids before Communion once or twice each week, the present law allows it daily. The Code law moreover demanded a sickness of such a serious nature that the patient had to be confined to his home, while the present law is much more lenient and favorable in that it merely demands a slight illness, such as that arising from a severe headache. Again, the present faculty may be used as soon as the person becomes sick, whereas the former privilege could not be used until the person had been sick for a month. In this regard it should be noted that the medicinal qualities of alcoholic beverages have been called into question in recent years and have for the most part been rejected by medical experts. Furthermore, as will be shown in a later chapter, medicines with an alcoholic base are allowed in the new legislation, so that the aggravated condition of the sick under the new law is really only an apparent one. As McReavy states, "the new law provides adequately for all categories of sick and infirm people." [16] These arguments are at least strong indications that the privilege in question has been revoked.

From an examination of the repealing clause of all former privileges and faculties in the Constitution it is difficut to see how anyone can still maintain that canon 858, § 2, is still in force. The Supreme Pontiff in the same sentence in which he promulgates the new law states that, "since all other privileges and faculties, no matter how granted by the Holy See, are abolished, We desire that everyone everywhere give due and proper observance to the new discipline." These words, so explicitly stating that all privileges and faculties no matter how granted are revoked, certainly include the faculties and privileges granted by the Code. For the law of canon 858, § 2, is certainly a privilege, and had the legislator intended to revoke only such as were granted *extra Codicem* he certainly would have said so. The only conclusion in keeping with the wording of the law as stated in the Constitution is that the legislator, when promulgating the new law, at the same time revoked the law of the Code except in those matters which reflect a repetition of

[16] Cf. "Correspondence," *The Clergy Review,* XXXVIII (1953), 575.

the Code law. In other words, with the promulgation of the Apostolic Constitution *Christus Dominus* comes a reorganization of the law of the Code regarding the Eucharistic fast. Hence, it must be concluded that canon 858, § 2, is repealed.

How, then, is the new law to be interpreted? In every interpretation of law the purpose is to ascertain its meaning according to the mind of the legislator.[17] This is accomplished through the application of the rules enacted in canon 18, namely that ecclesiastical laws are to be understood according to the proper juridical meaning of the words according to both text and context. It may happen, however, that even in the juridical sense a word may be used in a broad or narrow connotation. Thus, a broad interpretation is one in which a word is understood in that proper sense that has the greater extension, i.e., applies to more cases. A narrow interpretation, on the other hand, is one in which the word is understood in that proper sense that has the lesser extension, i.e., applies to fewer cases.[18]

From this it follows that neither broad nor strict interpretations go beyond the proper sense of the words. Though neither the Constitution nor the Instruction makes any reference to either broad or strict interpretations, nevertheless, interpretations are not ignored in either document. The Constitution itself makes one such reference: "Let Ordinaries of places carefully see to it that any interpretation which would amplify the faculties granted be avoided." [19]

In the Instruction there are five distinct references to interpretation, all however referring to amplification of the faculties granted.[20]

What precisely does the legislator mean by an amplification of the faculties? The meaning of *amplificare* is to make something larger than it is when the dimensions of the thing are known. In other words, there is an extension of the law to include cases

[17] Coronata, *Institutiones Iuris Canonici* (2. ed., 5 vols., Taurini—Romae: Marietti, 1939-1947), I, n. 22 (hereafter cited as *Institutiones*).

[18] Cf. Reed, "Select Questions on the Eucharistic Fast," *Theological Studies,* XVI (1955), 34.

[19] Cf. Apostolic Constitution, n. 31.

[20] Cf. Instruction, Introduction, n. 5, 10, 12, 19.

not intended by the words of the law.[21] A broad or a strict interpretation is demanded only when the meaning of the terms is not clearly known. Thus the legislator is simply prohibiting the extensions of those concessions whose limits are obvious, rather than the broad interpretation of terms which are doubtful in the text.

This fact is substantiated by the *Monitum* of the Sacred Congregation of the Holy Office of March 22, 1955.[22] In this document the Holy Office warned ordinaries against the granting of any permissions for evening Masses simply for the good of individuals or for the mere external adornment of some solemnity. It recalled to the minds of the bishops the words of the Apostolic Constitution which forbid any amplification of the faculties. However, it makes no reference to a liberal interpretation of them. Surely, if a liberal interpretation were regarded as an abuse, the Holy Office would have mentioned it in this recent *Monitum*. It must therefore be concluded that the Apostolic Constitution and the Instruction are to be interpreted according to the norms of interpretation enacted in canon 18, which in practice will mean a broad one.

Article 3. Its Relation to the Instruction of January 6, 1953.

One of the questions agitating the minds of canonists is the exact nature of the Instruction of the Holy Office of January 6, 1953. The precise question to be resolved is whether the Instruction gives preceptive norms or simply directive norms. In other words, was the Instruction aproved by the Sovereign Pontiff in *forma specifica,* or merely in *forma communi.*

The *Motu Proprio* of Pope Benedict XV, September 15, 1917, clearly sets forth the special character of Instructions. " The ordinary function of the Sacred Congregations as regards general decrees of this kind will be to see that the prescriptions of the Code are faithfully observed, and, if necessary, to issue Instructions that will bring out in clear light the precepts of the Code

[21] Cf. Michiels, *Normae Generales Iuris Canonici,* I, 480; Reed, " art. cit.," *ibid.*, p. 36.

[22] Cf. *AAS*, XLVII (1955), 218.

and make them more effective. These documents shall be drawn up in such a way that they not only are but also appear as specific explanations and complements of the canons, which therefore will most suitably be incorporated in the very text of the documents." [23]

From this it is evident that it is the function of such an Instruction to explain, illuminate, and complement the law, as well as to promote its execution. Does the present Instruction have merely such a purpose, or has it been approved in *forma specifica,* and thereby become Pontifical law? [24] The answer at first sight would seem to be in the negative, inasmuch as the usual expressions indicating approbation *in forma specifica* are lacking. However, the absence of such expressions as " motu proprio ", or " ex certa scientia ", do not constitute infallible proof that the Instruction has not been so approved.[25] The vast majority of canonists, however, while admitting that the usual expressions indicating approbation *in forma specifica* are absent, conclude that the Instruction in question has been so approved.[26]

[23] *AAS,* IX (1917), 483.

[24] For a thorough explanation of the phrase in *forma specifica* and in *forma communi* cf. Van Hove, *De Legibus Ecclesiasticis,* pp. 349 f.

[25] An Instruction which is approved only *in forma communi* may have the general character of a decree. Thus the Instruction of the Sacred Congregation of the Sacraments of December 21, 1930, on the examination of candidates for Sacred Orders, is a document whose directives must be observed exactly by ordinaries. *AAS,* XXII (1931), 120; cf. Schmidt, *The Principles of Authentic Interpretation in Canon 17 of the Code of Canon Law,* The Catholic University of America Canon Law Studies, n. 141 (Washington, D.C.: The Catholic University of America Press, 1941), p. 101.

[26] Cf. Conway, *The New Law on the Eucharistic Fast,* Text, Translation, Commentary (2. impression, Dublin: Brown and Nolan, 1955), p. 31 (hereafter cited as Conway); Coronata, *De Nova Disciplina Ieiunii Eucharistici et de Missis Vespertinis,* Commentarium in Constitutionem *Christus Dominus* et in Instructionem Sancti Officii, diei 6 Ianuarii, 1953 (Romae: Officium Libri Catholici, 1955), p. 22; Reed, "Select Questions on the Eucharistic Fast," *Theological Studies,* XVI (1955), 33; Ford, *The New Eucharistic Legislation,* A commentary on the Apostolic Constitution *Christus Dominus* and on the Instruction of the Holy Office on the Discipline to be observed concerning the Eucharistic Fast (2. ed. New York: Kenedy, 1955), p. 114 (hereafter cited as Ford); Moriarty, "New Regulations on the Eucharistic Fast," *The Jurist,* XIV (1954), 1-31.

Before reaching a conclusion in this matter, however, one should consider, as Van Hove pointed out, that an Instruction may be approved *in forma specifica* without any juridical form of approbation appearing in the text.[27] An examination of the Instruction reveals three things that cannot be overlooked in a deciding of its juridic nature. The first is the statement in the introductory paragraph that "this Supreme Congregation of the Holy Office, at the direction and by the command of the Supreme Pontiff himself, decrees as follows." This indicates that the Holy Office issued this particular Instruction in virtue of a special mandate from the Pope and not in virtue of its ordinary power of applying and supplementing the general law in specific cases. Not only did he direct the Congregation to write the Instruction, but he specified the rules that were to be contained in it.

In addition, as Father Hürth points out, the verb "*statuit*" in the same paragraph should be taken in its ordinary juridical sense as implying the constituting of a law rather than the supplying of an admonition. The Holy Office is not empowered to constitute law (*leges statuere*) unless this extraordinary faculty is granted to it by the Supreme Pontiff himself.

Finally, in approving the Instruction the Holy Father indicated the close bond that existed between the Apostolic Constitution and the Instruction. "The Sovereign Pontiff approving this Instruction, decreed that it should be promulgated by publication in *Acta Apostolica Sedis*, together with the Apostolic Constitution *Chrustus Dominus*." In other words, they were to appear side by side in the official Vatican publication on the same day as one law for the universal Church. Thus it seems that the Apostolic Constitution and the accompanying Instruction do not constitute two laws, but are one and the same law to be observed by all.[28]

[27] Cf. Van Hove, *op. cit.* p. 349.

[28] Cf. Hürth, *De Nova Disciplina Ieiunii Eucharistici,* Constitutio Apostolica *Christus Dominus* necnon Instructio SS. Oficii (6 ian. 1953), Textus et Commentarius (Romae: Pontificia Universitas Gregoriana, 1953), pp. 22. 23 (hereafter cited as Hürth).

CHAPTER II

GENERAL JURIDICAL NORMS

Article 1. The Notion of *Grave Incommodum*

It is evident from both the Apostolic Constitution and the Instruction that not every inconvenience entitles one to take liquid foods or medicine before Communion, but only the ones listed, namely, the celebration of Mass after nine o'clock, a walk of at least a mile and a quarter, infirmity, debilitating labor, and hard work in the ministry. Canonists are not in agreement, however, as to the precise meaning of the phrase *grave incommodum*. This much at least is certain that it is not the same as the English translation, which usually renders it as a grave inconvenience. Rather, it should be understood to mean any real, true, genuine inconvenience. This is evident from the fact that the official Italian translation published in *Acta Apostolicae Sedis* has " *senza vero incommodo* " in number one of the Instruction, and " *grave incommodo* " in numbers nine, ten, and eleven.[1]

Moreover, it has been the practice of the Apostolic See in the past to grant dispensations from the Eucharistic fast for any genuine inconvenience. Since the new legislation is intended to cover such cases in a uniform manner as well as to mitigate the rigor of the law, it seems that the present law does not demand more, since otherwise the purpose of the law could readily be defeated.[2] Again, moralists as well as canonists interpret *grave incommodum* to mean a moderately serious inconvenience rather than an absolutely grave one. These reasons are substantiated by the fact already shown, namely, that the new legislation is to be given a liberal interpretation whenever possible.

A more difficult problem, however, is to decide whether the

[1] *AAS*, XLV (1953), 52.

[2] Ford, pp. 51 ff.

legislator postulates a subjectively serious inconvenience on the part of the subjects, or simply one that in general can be classified objectively as such. Some commentators demand that the subjective inconvenience be verified in each case before any one is entitled to avail himself of the concessions. Others are of the opinion that one or the other of the circumstances or causes enumerated serve of themselves to beget the inconvenience, thus rendering the person a fit subject for the concessions, even though no inconvenience whatsoever is felt.

In solving this problem one must keep in mind that the text of the law cannot be separated from the context. In other words, as already shown, the Constitution and the Instruction must be taken as a unit, that is, as one law for the universal Church.

From the words of the text it seems that a real subjective inconvenience is necessary in every case. The first argument one may proffer is found in the Constitution, where the Holy Father, after recalling the history of the Eucharistic fast, introduces the question of its mitigation by this solemn warning:

> " It has seemed good to recall these facts to mind in order that all may recognize that We, although induced by the new conditions of affairs and of the times to grant not a few faculties and permissions in this matter, intend, nevertheless, by these Apostolic Letters to retain in full force the law and custom respecting the Eucharistic fast; and We wish, furthermore, to remind those who are able to obey this law, that they continue diligently to do so, so that only those who are in necessity may enjoy these concessions, according to the measure of that necessity." [3]

These words clearly indicate that the legislator is referring solely to subjective inconvenience, for the statement that " only those who are in necessity may enjoy these concessions " implicity excludes those who experience no such necessity. In addition the Sovereign Pontiff is here stating a principle governing the interpretation of the whole law, namely, that the concessions are granted only for those who really need them and can benefit by them.

The same need of subjective inconvenience is evident from

[3] Apostolic Constitution, n. 9.

the first norm of the Instruction referring to the sick. The faculty as there granted states that " the faithful who are sick, even though not confined to bed, can take something by way of drink, except alcoholic drinks, if by reason of their sickness they are unable to observe the complete fast until the reception of Holy Communion without grave inconvenience." [4] Here again the words of the law are obvious. The legislator states that the personal serious inconvenience is a *conditio sine qua non* for the use of the concession.

Some authors [5] see in the fifth norm of the Constitution a certain ambiguity likely to give the impression that the legislator is there referring to an objective inconvenience only.[6] It could be argued that the use of the words, " that is, because of exhausting labor," etc., in apposition to the phrase " grave inconvenience " suggests that the legislator indicates that one or the other of the causes mentioned will of themselves beget a grave inconvenience in every case. However, when this norm is considered in conjunction with its counterpart in the Instruction [7] the ambiguity vanishes. The wording of the Instruction is here so clear that it is difficult to understand why anyone should question its meaning.

The Instruction first states that a serious inconvenience must

[4] Instruction, n. 1.

[5] Genicot-Putz, " The Eucharistic Fast," *The Clergy Monthly,* XVII (1953) (Ranchi, India), p. 249. Reed, " Select Questions on the Eucharistic Fast," *Theological Studies,* XVI (1955), 44, 45.

[6] Cf. Norm V, n. 28: The faithful in like manner, even though not sick, who, because of grave inconvenience—that is, because of exhausting labor, or because they can draw near the Holy Banquet only at a rather late hour, or because of a long journey which they must make—cannot approach the Eucharistic table completely fasting, may with the prudent advice of a confessor, as long as the need lasts, take something by way of drink, exclusive of alcoholic beverages; they must abstain, however, from such drink at least for the space of one hour before they are nourished by the Bread of Angels.

[7] Instruction, n. 9; The faithful in like manner who are unable to observe the Eucharistic fast, not by reason of sickness but because of some other grave inconvenience, are allowed to take something by way of drink, except, however, alcoholic beverages, and provided they observe one hour's fast before the reception of Holy Communion.

be present,[8] and in the succeeding number it enumerates the causes of the inconvenience. It is significant, however, that the ambiguity here spoken of was contained also in the original text of the Instruction which appeared in *Osservatore Romano* on January 15, 1953. In that document there was the statement: "Casus in quibus grave incommodum habetur, tres enumerantur." Later the Sacred Congregation, in the final text which appeared in the *Acta Apostolicae Sedis,* changed it to read: "Causae gravis incommodi tres enumerantur." Reed argues that the reason for changing the original text was simply the achieving of greater clarity, inasmuch as the document listed three generic headings of inconvenience (work, journey, late hour) to which the word "*casus*" was not properly applicable.[9]

It seems much more likely that the change was made because the words were found misleading and therefore could be regarded as of themselves enabling a person to enjoy the concession. To forestall that consequence the legislator changed the wording of the law. The meaning of the text is now quite clear. It simply states that the causes of the serious inconvenience are threefold, so that, when one or the other of the causes is verified in a particular instance, it is to be presumed that a serious subjective inconvenience is also present. But like all presumptions of law, this presumption gives way to truth.

This view is corroborated by another fact, namely, that the faithful cannot avail themselves of this faculty without the prudent advice of a confessor. He is to make a prudent judgment, having considered not merely whether one or the other of the three causes is present, but also having taken into account the age of the person, the strength of the individual, etc. Only then is he to decide whether the required subjective inconvenience is present. Otherwise, why demand the advice of a confessor? Undoubtedly, such a condition as a journey of a mile and a quarter, or a late hour interpreted by the Instruction as nine o'clock, could be determined and verified by the average person without

[8] Instruction, n. 9.

[9] "Select Questions on the Eucharistic Fast," *Theological Studies,* XVI (1955), 45.

any advice from a confessor had the legislator decided that these in themselves sufficed.

The counter argument adduced by Reed,[10] namely, that the burden for the faithful of deciding for themselves whether one or the other of the postulated conditions was really present would give rise to scruples, does not appear to carry any weight. If that were true, then the application of the majority of human laws would be an occasion for scruples. Moreover, when the confessor is consulted, the burden of deciding whether the inconvenience is present or not rests primarily with the individual; the confessor simply makes a prudent judgment on the facts as presented to him by the subject.

Moreover, it does not seem admissible that an insistence on subjective inconvenience in every case would cause a diversity of practice and thus would defeat the purpose of the law.[11] It is true that what might seem a real inconvenience to one person might be regarded as a very slight inconvenience to another. This the legislator foresaw, but he forestalled all likely inequalities by demanding that the prudent advice of a confessor be had in each case before the concessions be put into use. Confessors trained in the sacred sciences, when judging all the circumstances of the cases presented to them, are more likely to achieve a uniformity of practice than if it were left to the discretion of each individual to decide whether a serious subjective inconvenience is present.

Finally, some authors[12] attempt to constitute an argument from the fact that the law should be identical for priests and laity. They base their argument on the fact that the law seems to imply that priests can avail themselves of the faculty without any subjective inconvenience whenever one or the other of the stated causes is present. This argument is indefensible. There is no reason to believe that priests can use the faculty without any subjective inconvenience, for, as is stated in the Constitu-

[10] *Ibid.*, p. 49.

[11] Constitution, n. 22.

[12] Cf., e.g., Reed, *ibid.*, p. 50.

tion,[13] "only those who are in necessity may enjoy these concessions according to the measure of that necessity."

Again, a consideration of numbers 12 and 13 of the Constitution, where the legislator treats of the reasons which prompted him to mitigate the law for priests also, implies that a serious inconvenience must be present in their cases even though that is not expressly so stated. This view is corroborated by a private reply from the Holy Office on January 23, 1953. This reply states that "priests who have a physical condition so robust as not to feel any grave inconvenience from prolonged fasting cannot avail themselves of the concessions made by the Holy Father in the Apostolic Constitution *Christus Dominus,* even though they have to celebrate Mass at a late hour, or at a distant place, since the obligation of the Eucharistic fast is mitigated for those persons only who cannot observe it fully."[14]

Article 2. The Notion of a Confessor

The very notion of the word confessor brings to mind the idea of jurisdiction, which connotes the public power of ruling and of guiding the faithful with a view to their eternal salvation.[15] This power is twofold, depending on its relation either to the external forum, which governs the individual's relation to the common good of the whole visible society, or to the internal forum, which governs the individual's moral actions in their relation to God for his own private welfare. All ecclesiastical jurisdiction by reason of the title on which it is based is either ordinary or delegated. The former is that which is attached to an office by the law; the latter is that which is committed to a person.[16]

Canon 872 repeats the traditional teaching of the Church regarding a confessor, namely, that he is one who in addition to possessing the power of orders also enjoys either ordinary or delegated jurisdiction over the subject. The canons and canon-

[13] Cf. n. 9.

[14] Bouscaren, *The Canon Law Digest* (3 vols., and Supplements through 1955, Milwaukee: Bruce, 1934, 1943, 1953, and 1954-1956), Supplement, under canon 808.

[15] Ottaviani, *Institutiones Iuris Publici Ecclesiastici* (2 vols. in 1, Romae: Apud Aedes Facultatis Iuridicae ad S. Apollinaris, 1925), n. 112.

[16] Can. 197, § 1.

ists of the Oriental as well as of the Latin Church stated these same requirements long before the promulgation of the Latin Code. Theodore Balsamon (ca. 1140-ca. 1195) declared that in the Church of the East only priests who had the permission of the bishop could hear confessions.[17]

The collections of Gratian († ca. 1157) and of Bernard of Pavia († 1213) [18] give ample evidence of the same doctrine of the Church in the West. In an effort to refute the erroneous teaching of the Protestant Reformation, the Council of Trent found it necessary to define in express terms what had been the traditional doctrine concerning the nature of sacramental absolution and the necessity of confessional jurisdiction.[19] The Council taught that sacramental absolution partakes of the nature of a judicial act. Since the confessor acts as a judge within the sacred tribunal of penance, he must have the authority necessary to pronounce sentence. To give valid sacramental absolution, therefore, every confessor must possess judicial jurisdiction in the internal sacramental forum.

Like so many questions in the Constitution, the word confessor in the statement "*causae quidem gravis incommodi sunt prudenter a confessario pensitandae in foro interno sacramentali vel non sacramentali*" has been the subject of much discussion. There does not seem to be any general agreement among commentators on whether the confessor must have actual jurisdiction over the person consulting him. Three distinct views have been put forward on this subject, none of which are free from objections. The first, and by far the most widely held, demands that the priest who is consulted must have confessional faculties,

[17] Fonti, Serie II, Fasc. V, *Textus Selecti ex Operibus Commentatorum Byzantinorum Iuris Ecclesiastici* (Romae: Typis Polyglottis Vaticanis, 1939), n. 404; Cf. also Walsh, *The Jurisdiction of the Interritual Confessor in the United States and Canada,* The Catholic University of America Canon Law Studies, n. 320 (Washington, D.C.: The Catholic University of America Press, 1950), p. 28 (hereafter cited as Walsh).

[18] Cf. c. 2, C. IX, q. 2; *Dictum* ad c. 19, C. XVI, q. 1; c. 3, D. VI, *de poenit.;* Bernardus Papiensis, *Summa Decretalium* (ed. E. A. Th. Laspeyres, Ratisbonae, 1860), Lib. V, tit. XXXIII, n. 5.

[19] Sess. XIV, *de poenitentia,* c. 7; also can. 9; sess. XXII, *de ref.,* c. 15; also cf. Walsh, p. 29.

valid specifically for the person seeking the advice.[20] The second opinion would allow a priest when he has limited faculties here and now to advise those persons whose confessions he could not validly hear in virtue of those faculties, e.g., women religious.[21] The third view maintains that the faithful can be advised in this regard by any priest who enjoys at least limited faculties in some territory, even though he has none in the territory where he is consulted.[22]

Since canon 872 states that the power of jurisdiction as well as the power of orders is essential to the notion of a confessor, it follows that as a minimum requirement the priest whose counsel is sought must have some habitual faculties. The relevant question, therefore, can be reduced to this: must the confessor have actual jurisdiction? If jurisdiction is demanded, then it follows that the person seeking the advice must approch a priest who could hear his confession here and now. If jurisdiction is not demanded, then there is no reason for saying that the confessor who is approached for advice needs to have faculties in one region rather than in another.

Now, jurisdiction is twofold, that is, judicial and voluntary, and the jurisdiction enjoyed by a confessor is judicial. However, the exercise of a judicial delegated jurisdiction outside the confines of one's territory is invalid. But the new legislation demands the advice of a confessor in every case, for the Instruction states: " Nor can the faithful who are not fasting receive the Most Holy Eucharist without his advice.[23] Therefore, there seems demanded the advice of a priest who has jurisdiction to hear the confession of the person seeking advice, should the latter decide to go here and now. Furthermore, a priest is not a confessor in a territory where he enjoys no jurisdiction.

But even though one were to admit that the confessor men-

20 Hürth, pp. 29-30; Conway, p. 38.

21 Castellano, "Ad novam disciplinam circa jejunium Eucharisticum commentarium ", *Monitor Ecclesiasticus,* LXXVIII (1953), 398-399.

22 Connell, " The New Rules for the Eucharistic Fast ", *The American Ecclesiastical Review,* CXXVIII (1953), 248 (hereafter abbreviated *AER*).

23 Cf. n. 11.

tioned here is a confessor even in the broadest sense, nevertheless the succeeding phrase in the text limits it by stating that the causes of the inconvenience must be pondered by the confessor in the sacramental or non-sacramental internal forum. Had the law stated that the advice could be given " in or outside confession " it could be argued that jurisdiction is not necessary, but that possibility is removed by the mention of the internal forum whether sacramental or non-sacramental. In other words, the confessor must give his advice at least in the non-sacramental forum, thus exempting the subject from the necessity of confession. Moreover, the word forum implies and connotes jurisdiction, for in the absence of jurisdiction there is no forum. As Conway states, the very notion of the internal forum postulates a jurisdictional link between the confessor and the person consulting him. If that jurisdictional link does not exist, the advice sought and received is not an event in the internal forum, but merely a private conversation.[24]

This opinion is corroborated by a private reply from the Holy Office to a query from the Episcopal Curia of Trieste-Capodistria: " The confessor of whom mention is made in numbers 2 and 11 of the Instruction can be any priest who has the faculty to hear the confession of the person who applies to him, even if the person has not confessed to him and does not now do so." [25] Thus it seems that the law intends by the word confessor to mean a priest who here and now could hear the confession of the person seeking advice, should that person decide to go to confession.

While this opinion seems to be the one most in keeping with the wording of the law, it cannot be denied that, like the two other views, it also has its difficulties. At first sight it seems a rather strict interpretation when applied to extreme cases. An example will help to illustrate the difficulty. In the United States an assistant priest usually receives faculties to absolve penitents of either sex with the exception of women religious. According to the opinion stated above, such a confessor could

[24] *The New Law on the Eucharistic Fast,* p. 38.

[25] Bouscaren, *The Canon Law Digest,* Supplement under canon 858.

not give the required advice to a woman religious who might approach him. However, in answer to such an objection it might be stated that the law [26] gives the required faculties to such a confessor when the religious wishes to confess for peace of conscience. Now, if the law supplies faculties in such a case for the internal sacramental forum, *a fortiori* it should supply them in the internal non-sacramental one. This, however, is not the case. But it does not seem to be stretching the law too far to state that such a confessor could give the required advice both lawfully and validly.

Closely allied to the foregoing problem is the question of giving the required advice by letter, or by telephone, or through a third party. The first thing to be remembered here is that the advice is demanded so that the confessor, having heard the reasons, may make a prudent judgment whether the postulated subjective inconvenience is present. To do this by mail, telephone or through the medium of a third party would be virtually impossible. Even when the subject is present the making of such a judgment is difficult, and the confessor will at times be forced to give the subject the benefit of the doubt when he has failed to obtain moral certainty.

Secondly, confessors in utilizing such media are likely to make decisions for persons who are outside their territory and over whom they have no jurisdiction. Such advice would undoubtedly be given ineffectively because, as has already been shown, judicial jurisdiction cannot be exercised outside one's own territory.[27] Moriarty [28] points out that in the case of children a consultation of the confessor by their parents provides an even more effective safeguard of the law inasmuch as children could not draw the necessary line of demarcation between liquid and solid food. Obviously, this is not the point at issue. Nobody denies that parents are more qualified than children for so doing, but this is not the decision required from the confessor. Rather, he must decide if one or the other of the necessary conditions

[26] Can. 572.

[27] Can. 201, § 2.

[28] "New Regulations on the Eucharistic Fast", *The Jurist,* XIV (1954), 24.

and the required serious inconvenience arising therefrom is present.

Some authors[29] maintain that, since one can obtain a dispensation from fast or abstinence through the medium of a third party from a priest who has the power to grant the dispensation in the internal extra-sacramental forum, the same should hold in regard to the Eucharistic fast. While there definitely seems to be a parallel between the two cases, the fact must always be kept in mind that one of the principal reasons for this new legislation was to beget uniformity of practice throughout the universal Church. This the legislator intended to accomplish by requiring the prudent advice of a confessor who would reach a prudent judgment after considering all the circumstances in every case. It is well nigh impossible to reach a prudent judgment about the subjective condition of a person by way of a conversation on the telephone, or by means of a letter, or through a third party. Moreover, the mention of the confessor in the internal extra-sacramental forum, which implies that the subject does not necessarily have to go to confession every time the advice is needed, is a further indication that the legislator did not want such media as the telephone, letters, etc., used for the ascertaining of the necessary advice.

In addition, the new law is a rather complex and difficult one. Not only must the confessor decide whether the requisite serious inconvenience is present, but he must take account of several other intricacies of the law, such as the notion of alcohol, the notion of liquids, the notion of medicine, etc. To make a prudent judgment on these matters would be rather difficult for the average person, and it would be equally difficult for the confessor to do so by means of the mails, or by telephone, or through a third person. This view is substantiated by a private reply of the Holy Office to the query from the Curia of the diocese of Trieste-Capodistria on February 11, 1953. The reply stated that the confessor cannot give the required advice in writing, nor by telephone, nor through a third party.[30] This reply, while not a definitive one, cannot be disregarded, for the Instruction was is-

[29] Genicot-Putz, p. 256.

[30] Bouscaren, *The Canon Law Digest,* Supplement under canon 858.

sued by the Holy Office, which alone is competent regarding all matters concerning the Eucharistic fast.[31]

If, then, the advice may not be given by means of the telephone, nor by letter, nor through a third party, what is to be thought of the opinion which maintains that a presumed permission may be put into use whenever recourse to a confessor is difficult or impossible? Genicot-Putz [32] think that it is a probable and safe opinion to presume the confessor's advice in such circumstances. Werts [33] maintains a similar opinion. Connell [34] says the advice of the confessor binds only *sub levi,* and thus could be presumed in a particular case. He bases this view on the fact that Cappello interpreted the privilege of canon 858, § 2, in such a way that the advice of the confessor mentioned therein could in certain circumstances be assumed.

First of all, the text of the new law seems to be much more strict than the privilege mentioned in canon 858, § 2. While the law in canon 858 merely demands the prudent advice of the confessor, the present law goes farther: in two different instances it states not only that the advice of the confessor is necessary but also that it is expressly forbidden to use the concessions without consultation.[35] Had the legislator simply stated that the concessions were made available with the prudent advise of the confessor, it could be argued that as in canon 858, § 2, there was some room for presuming the advice in certain circumstances, but that possibility is excluded by the statements which forbid anyone to use the concessions until the advice has been obtained. Moreover, as Michiels shows, permission cannot be presumed when express permission is demanded by the law itself.[36] Fur-

[31] Can. 247, § 5: Ipsa una competens est circa ea omnia quae ieiunium eucharisticum pro sacerdotibus Missam celebrantibus respiciunt.

[32] *Ibid.*, p. 257.

[33] "The Eucharistic Fast," *Review for Religious,* XII (1953), 308.

[34] "The New Rules for the Eucharistic Fast," *AER,* CXXVIII (1953), 248.

[35] Instruction, n. 2, states: "The conditions must be prudently weighed by a confessor, nor can anyone use the dispensation without his advice." Similarly n. 11 states: ". . . nor can the faithful who are not fasting receive the Most Holy Eucharist without his advice."

[36] *Normae Generales*, II, 681.

thermore, when a permission is presumed by the individual it is the latter who judges the lawfulness of his act the while he presumes that his superior would approve it; in reality, however, the making of the requisite judgment lies outside the individual's power completely.

Again, it is a principle of ecclesiastical jurisprudence that the laws which are enacted as safeguards against a common danger must be observed, even though there is no danger in a particular case.[37] Can it be argued that this is such a law? And, if it be so, what is the danger envisioned? It seems that this can be such a law if two facts are considered.

In the first place, the purpose of the whole new legislation was to beget uniformity of practice. Secondly, the purpose of demanding the advice of the confessor in every case was to prevent abuses. As already shown, if each individual were permitted to use his own judgment in place of being required to consult a confessor in every case, a diversity of practice would soon arise, the very thing the legislator intended to prevent and forestall. Undoubtedly, also, some persons would avail themselves of the concessions when the required conditions are not present, for not every individual is capable of making a prudent judgment in the application of so complex a law. Hence, it seems that the legislator had two abuses in mind when he enacted the present legislation: first, the one already prevalent, namely, a lack of uniformity in the application of the law of the Eucharistic fast as arising from a multiplicity of indults, and, secondly, the emergence of the same abuse from the present law if each individual were to decide in his own case whether the requisite conditions are present.

Furthermore, he foresaw that some would be availing themselves of the concessions even when not entitled to them. Thus it seems that the present law was enacted for the preventing of a common danger, and as such always binds, so that a presumed permission is never justified. This opinion is corroborated by the statement made by Hürth: "*Licentia praesumpta* non videtur admittenda, certo non in casu in quo confessarius adiri potest; sed neque in aliis casibus, quia periculum est nimis mag-

[37] Canon 21 states: "Leges latae ad praecavendum periculum generale, urgent, etiamsi in casu peculiari periculum non adsit."

num, ne intenta a Legislatore vigilantia Ecclesiae circa concessi indulti usum illusoria reddatur." [38] However, laws which are enacted for the prevention of a common danger, like all other positive laws, do not bind when their observance would entail a positive harm. In other words, one may be excused from its observance, given a proportionate cause. Thus, if there should arise a situation wherein the consultation of a confessor would cause positive harm, one would be excused from the obligation of the law.[39]

Closely allied to the foregoing problem is the question of giving the required advice to a group of persons who are in the same set of circumstances when it is manifest that the serious inconvenience exists for each member of the group. Genicot-Putz [40] Bride,[41] Connell [42] and Ford,[42a] are of the opinion that this is lawful as long as the confessor knows that the conditions are verified in each case.

It must be admitted that it seems incongruous that a priest should have to give individual advice to each of the pupils in a large parochial school. However, two things must be observed. In the first place, the law demands that no lay person take advantage of the concessions without having first of all consulted a confessor in the internal forum,[43] and it would seem farfetched to consider a priest giving advice from the pulpit or addressing a large group of children in a parochial school as prudently pondering the peculiar circumstances of each individual in the internal forum. Secondly, in demanding the advice of the

38 *De Nova Disciplina Ieiunii Eucharistici,* p. 31.

39 Reed, p. 60.

40 "The Eucharistic Fast," *The Clergy Monthly,* XVII (1953), 256.

41 "Jeûne Eucharistique: Discipline Nouvelle," *L'Ami du Clergé,* LXIII (1953), 206.

42 "The New Rules for the Eucharistic Fast," *AER,* CXXVIII (1953), 252.

42a "*The New Eucharistic Legislation*", p. 67.

43 Cf. Instruction, n. 11, where it is stated: "The causes of the grave inconvenience are to be prudently pondered by a confessor in the sacramental or non-sacramental internal forum; nor can the faithful who are not fasting receive the Most Holy Eucharist without his advice."

confessor in each case the legislator intended to prevent abuses and to beget uniformity, neither of which could be achieved by way of a group consultation.

Again, as has already been shown, the law postulates a subjective inconvenience in every case. While it may be admitted that the serious subjective inconvenience will be present in the vast majority of cases, nevertheless there may be some who do not experience such inconvenience, and these would be violating the law. Moreover, as Conway states,[44] every human law creates difficulties and anomalies which seem unreasonable, but such difficulties do not justify the violation of a law. Finally, the confessor is to examine each particular case in the internal forum, and only when he has found out that the postulated subjective inconvenience is present will he make the required decision. This he can achieve only by means of a face to face consultation, as is evident from the word " perpendere." [45]

Article 3. The Notion of Natural Water

From the earliest times the law of the Eucharistic fast was identical with the natural fast, the two terms being as it were synonymous. St. Augustine (354-430) tried to show that the law of the Eucharistic fast was instituted by St. Paul, and therefore was of Apostolic origin.[46] In a later day St. Thomas clarified the notion of food by stating that the criterion to be adopted in determining whether a given substance fulfilled the notion of food, drink, or medicine, was its digestibility. The nutritive or non-nutritive qualities were not considered.[47]

Theologians and canonists in the past agreed that the nature and the digestibility of a given substance were to be judged by the common estimation of men and through the findings of chem-

[44] *The New Law on the Eucharistic Fast,* p. 41.

[45] Instruction, n. 11.

[46] C. 54. D, II, *de cons.;* Epistula XIV, (ad Januarium)—Migne, *Patrologiae Cursus Completus,* Series Latina (221 vols., Parisiis: 1844-1864), XXXIII, 203.

[47] Cf. *Summa Theologica,* Pars III, q. LXXX, a. 8: " Nec refert utrum aliquid huiusmodi nutriat vel non nutriat aut per se aut cum aliis, dummodo sumatur per modum cibi vel potus."

istry, and that in a case of doubt the preference rested on the side of the common estimation of men.[48] The Code of Canon Law again identifies the natural fast and the Eucharistic fast.[49]

The present legislation, however, omits all reference to the natural fast for the obvious reason that it decrees as a general principle that natural water no longer breaks the Eucharistic fast.[50] The concept of natural water is described in the Instruction. It states that it is water without the addition of any element whatsoever.[51] Now, the notion of natural water according to this description may give rise to doubt in the minds of some. Does the legislator wish to exclude every addition, even those made by nature as well as those made by the civil authority for the protection of the health of the citizens?

Here the legislator is referring to additions made by human endeavour, for the Constitution treats of natural water. According to the rule already stated, water to which nature has added something, such as the natural mineral content in the water, would still in the common estimation of men be regarded as natural water.[52] Thus it may be stated that mineral water, that is, water which in its natural state contains even a consider-

[48] Cf. Anglin, *The Eucharistic Fast,* The Catholic University of America Canon Law Studies, n. 124 (Washington, D.C.: The Catholic University of America Press, 1941), p. 63 (hereafter cited as Anglin); Regatillo-Zalba, *Theologiae Moralis Summa* (3 vols., Matriti: Biblioteca de Autores Cristianos, 1952-1954), III, n. 127; Noldin-Schmidt, *Summa Theologiae Moralis* (26. ed. 3 vols., Oeniponte-Lipsiae, 1940), III, *De Sacramentis,* n. 149; Cappello, *Tractatus Canonico-Moralis de Sacramentis,* Vol. I, *De Sacramentis in Genere, de Baptismo, Confirmatione et Eucharistiae* (2. ed., Romae: Marietti, 1928), n. 503.

[49] Can. 808.—Sacerdoti celebrare ne liceat nisi ieiunio naturali a media nocte servato.

Can. 858, § 1.—Qui a media nocte ieiunium naturale non servaverit, nequit ad sanctissimam Eucharistiam admitti, nisi mortis urgeat periculum, aut necessitas impediendi irreverentiam in sacramentum.

[50] Apostolic Constitution, n. 24, Norm I: "But in future this shall be a general principle common to all, whether priests or faithful; namely, natural water does not break the fast."

[51] Cf. Introduction of the Instruction.

[52] Cf. Hürth, p. 25.

able quantity of minerals, may be taken without a breaking of the fast. On the other hand, manufactured mineral water may not be used, because here something has been added by human endeavour, so that the resulting liquid would not fulfill the idea of natural water to which nothing has been added.[53] Again, distilled water may be used unless in the process of distillation something has been added. The same is true of rain water, as well as of the water obtained from the melting of ice and snow.

As regards additions made by human endeavor, any substance that satisfies the notion of digestibility is forbidden. In modern times in urban communities it is difficult to find water to which nothing of a digestible nature has been added, inasmuch as the public health authorities as a general rule add some purifying substance to the water supply for the protection of the health of the citizens. Thus, it could seem that tap-water would not fulfill the description of natural water as set down in the Instruction. Yet all canonists agree that such water may be used. They base their contention on the fact that such water would in the common estimation of men fulfill the idea of natural water. Here, however, this criterion does not stand the test, for, as Conway states,[54] water to which a small quantity of salt has been added would also fulfill this requirement. On the basis of *epikeia*, or through a benign interpretation of the law, it seems that tap-water may be used, since otherwise the concessions would not benefit the vast majority of people, and the purpose of the law would be defeated.

What then is to be thought of the opinion advocated by Felici,[55] who believes that a private individual may apply the mixture for the purpose of purifying the water. This view seems reasonable, especially in regions where this practice is customary and where good water is not otherwise obtainable. It does not seem to matter whether the purifying substance is added by public or private authority. If this opinion cannot be sustained,

[53] Cf. Conway, p. 32.

[54] *The New Law on the Eucharistic Fast*, p. 32.

[55] Cf. "De nova ieiunii disciplina praecipue quoad fideles," *Apollinaris*, XXVIII (1955), 167.

then many of the faithful, especially in Continental countries, could not profit by the concessions, even though otherwise they would be entitled to them.

Genicot-Putz [56] believe that soda water can be classified as natural water, inasmuch as the gas added has not the nature of food or of drink, and in any case if the water is stirred or allowed to stand for a short period of time the gas escapes. Here, however, a distinction should be made. If gas alone is added, the resulting product still retains the notion of natural water. But if the gas is added by means of joining it with other digestible chemicals, then the resulting substance is not water to which nothing has been added, in line with the provision incorporated in the Instruction.

Article 4. The Notion of Liquid

The phrase *per modum potus,* as used in the Constitution [57] and in the Instruction,[58] is not a new one, but dates back to pre-Code jurisprudence. The Sacred Congregation of the Holy Office on September 7, 1897, explained the meaning of the phrase [59] by stating that it could include broth, coffee, or other liquid food in which there is mixed some substance such as semolina, crumbled bread, etc., as long as the mixture does not lose its character of liquid food. Again, in the Code of Canon Law [60] the same phrase is used, and yet there does not seem to be complete agreement among moralists and canonists as to its precise meaning.

[56] Cf. "The Eucharistic Fast," *The Clergy Monthly,* XVII (1953), 249-250.

[57] Cf. n. 25, Norm II.

[58] Cf. n. 1.

[59] "N.N. espone che egli ottenne a causa di cronica malattia la facoltà di prendere qualche ristoro *per modum potus* prima della Comunione. Aggravatosi vie più il suo male, e non bastandogli solo delle bevande, supplica la S.V. che si degni permettergli anche qualche cosa di solido per sostentarsi.

R. Respondeatur ad mentem, ut in Abellinen., 4 Iunii 1893: 'La mente è che quando si dice *per modum potus* s'intende bensì che si possa prendere brodo, caffè, od altro cibo liquido, in cui sia mescolata qualche sostanza, come p.e. semmolino [sic], pangrattato, ecc., purchè l'insieme non venga a perdere la natura di cibo liquido.' SSm̃us adprobavit".—*Fontes,* n. 1192.

[60] Can. 858, § 2.

First of all it should be noted that the meaning of liquids in the present context should not be confused with the liquids allowed between meals on fast days without a violating of the fast. Here the purpose of the liquids is to provide nourishment for a person unable to observe the Eucharistic fast, while the liquids permitted between meals on fast days are allowed to give the fasting person a certain stimulation that enables him to continue the fast. The liquids allowed between meals on fast days have little nutritive value, while the purpose of taking liquid in the new legislation is to provide nutrition. Hence, it seems that there is no limit to the amount of nutrition for which allowance is made in the new legislation.

Bride [61] and Conway [62] hold the contrary opinion. They believe that the phrase *aliquid sumere per modum potus,* when considered in the light of the former statement in the Constitution, "that only those in necessity may enjoy these concessions according to the measure of their necessity," [63] allows only a moderate amount of liquid food, or simply what proves sufficient to relieve the inconvenience. In answer to this it should be stated that the word *aliquid* points to something completely indefinite and is not a word that implies any positive limitation in and of itself. Furthermore, the Instruction [64] allows priests to take medicine or liquid food once or several times. Again, such a limitation as that of demanding that people measure the quantity of their food by their need would beget scrupulosity. While it would be the more perfect method of putting the concessions in use, and more in keeping with the spirit of the law, it does not seem to be demanded by the legislator.

How, then, is the phrase *per modum potus* to be interpreted? It seems that here again recourse must be had to the common estimation of men. Hürth [65] believes that a liquid is any substance which according to common parlance is said to be drunk

61 "Jeûne eucharistique: Discipline nouvelle," *L'Ami du Clergé,* LXIII (1953), 204.

62 *The New Law on the Eucharistic Fast,* pp. 41-42.

63 Cf. n. 9.

64 Cf. n. 9.

65 *De Nova Disciplina Ieiunii Eucharistici,* p. 27.

rather than eaten. This seems to be the most acceptable opinion, although it also has its weaknesses. Soup according to common usage is said to be eaten, yet all commentators admit that soup may be consumed by those who are entitled to the use of the concessions. Secondly, in any determining of a liquid or of something taken *per modum potus* it appears that the substance should be considered in its natural state, that is, as it appears immediately before being placed in the mouth. Thus, ice cream is undoubtedly a solid, and is usually spoken of as being eaten, not as something being drunk. In the same way lozenges are solids and may not be taken. However, medicated lozenges such as cough drops may be used, for they can be regarded as medicine which may be taken in either liquid or solid form.[66]

Werts[67] believes that anything that is capable of being poured and drunk may be used within the meaning of the phrase. However, this seems to be extending the meaning of the term liquid, and while other substances such as porridge may be poured, they would not be regarded as liquids in the common estimation of men. He also states that a lightly boiled egg may be used, but again it is not commonly regarded as a liquid. However, it does seem that heavier liquids, such as eggnog or milk shakes, may be used even though some undissolved solids remain in them, provided of course that the substance can be regarded as a potable liquid. This seems in keeping with the reply of the Holy Office[68] quoted above, which allowed crumbled bread in soup provided the resultant substance retained its liquid nature.[69]

Article 5. The Notion of Medicine

The new legislation allows the sick to take medicine in either liquid or solid form, whether prescribed by a doctor or taken on one's own initiative. It merely demands that the used substance be regarded as medicine in the common estimation of men.[70]

66 Instruction, n. I.

67 "The Eucharistic Fast," *Review for Religious*, XII (1953), 307.

68 *Fontes*, n. 1192.

69 Cf. Anglin, p. 138.

70 Instruction, n. I: ". . dummodo de vera medicina agatur, a medico praescripta vel uti tali vulgo recepta."

Thus, aspirin or digestive tablets are true medicine as also are sleeping pills.

In the Instruction there is, however, one expression concerning medicine which merits special consideration. It is there stated that not every solid taken as nourishment can be considered medicine.[71] Apparently, the legislator is referring to cases wherein a doctor would prescribe certain foods not for the purpose of nourishment but rather for medicinal reasons. Bride,[72] Werts [73] and Ford [74] believe that solid food may be regarded as a medicine when prescribed by a doctor. At first sight this view seems reasonable, for the legislation excludes food *qua* nourishment and not food *qua* medicine. However the contrary opinion seems more in keeping with the purpose of the law. The legislator appears to want to exclude solid food completely, and it would be extremely difficult for the average person to draw the line between cases wherein such solids are taken as nourishment and cases wherein they are taken as medicine. In reply to this it would be of no avail to say that the doctor's prescription would determine this, for the law does not demand a doctor's opinion.

Again, this practice would give rise to abuses which the law expressly wishes to prevent.[75] As Hürth states, solid food is excluded because the legislator did not wish to extend the indult to include such medicine.[76] Moreover, the Instruction [77] allows " true medicine either liquid or solid, as long as there is question tion of true medicine, prescribed by a physician, or commonly accepted as such." From these words it is difficult to see how food prescribed by a doctor can be regarded as true medicine.

[71] Instruction, n. I.

[72] Cf. "art. cit.," p. 204.

[73] Cf. " art. cit.," p. 308.

[74] Cf. *The New Eucharistic Legislation,* pp. 78-79.

[75] Cf. Instruction, Introduction.

[76] Cf. *op. cit.,* p. 28: "A 'medicina' autem excluditur quodlibet solidum pro nutrimento sumptum; non quia solidum nutrimentum non possit revera in determinatis casibus pro determinatis infirmis habere rationem verae medicinae, sed quia Legislator ad talem medicinam non vult extendere indultum, infirmis concessum.

[77] Cf. n. I.

While it may remedy the illness in some cases, it could hardly be said to be true medicine in the everyday meaning of the term. Nor can it be said to be medicine in the common estimation of men, thus fulfilling the requirement that it be "commonly accepted as such."

Furthermore, the statement in the Instruction,[78] "Advertendum autem est, non posse tamquam medicina haberi quodlibet solidum pro nutrimento sumptum," is subject to a twofold rendering. It could mean that not every solid taken as nourishment can be considered medicine,[79] implying that some may be real medicine, or, that no solid taken for nourishment can be held to be medicine.[80] If the latter is preferred—and there seems to be some justification for it—then there can be no doubt that solid food is completely forbidden even when taken as medicine, and even with the doctor's advice. This view is corroborated by the translation rendered by Bouscaren.[81]

Article 6. The Use of Alcohol

Among the disputed points in the new legislation is the proper interpretation of the phase "*exclusis alcoholicis,*" as found both in the Constitution[82] and in the Instructions.[83] In the first place, it should be noted that the evident purpose of the exclusion of alcohol throughout the law is the prevention of irreverance to Christ in the Eucharist. It is undeniable that there is a danger that some persons might approach the Table of the Lord in a state of alcoholic disturbance. This purpose should definitely prove a help in the interpretation of passages wherein the exact extent of the exclusion is doubtful in the words of the law. It can be stated at the outset that little help can be found

78 Cf. n. I.

79 Ford's translation, n. I. p. 31.

80 Conway's translation, *op. cit.*, p. 21.

81 Cf. Bouscaren, *Canon Law Digest,* Supplement, under Canon 858: "It must be noted, however, that any solid taken as nourishment cannot be considered as medicine."

82 Cf. n. 25, Norm II, and n. 26, Norm III.

83 Cf. Norm I and Norm IV.

in the text itself, for the simple reason that the phrase which excludes alcohol in the Instruction modifies the word "*liquidum,*" while in the Constitution in Norm II it modifies the word medicine.[84]

The majority of the commentators are agreed that the phrase "*exclusis alcoholicis*" applies to both parts of the concession, that is to say, alcohol may not be taken either as a drink or as a medicine. This is true whether taken as the result of a doctor's prescription, or on one's own initiative. Moriarty [85] believes that when a doctor prescribes an ounce of brandy or whiskey for a person suffering from heart disease, that is to say, when the patient takes the alcohol for medicinal purposes rather than for their alcoholic content, such a person could still go to Communion, provided of course that the other conditions were fulfilled. Reed [86] states that "while no one could be allowed to take alcoholic drinks on his own initiative, even under the guise of medicine, it is not so clear that the law intended to exclude from the benefits enjoyed by the rest of the sick those relatively rare cases in which a doctor may have prescribed a small dose of some form of alcohol (about one ounce as usual) as the one direct remedy for a heart condition." It is extremely difficult to see how this view can be reconciled with the words of the second Norm of the Constitution, wherein it is stated that the sick can take something by way of drink or of true medicine, except alcoholic beverages. These words expressly exclude alcoholic beverages even when taken as a medicine, and yet the author states that such beverages may be taken. Such an opinion is not merely a liberal interpretation of the law, it is also an extensive one, which is expressly forbidden.[87]

[84] Instruction, n. I, reads: " . . possunt etiam aliquid sumere per modum medicinae, sive liquidum (exclusis alcoholocis), sive solidum; Constitution, Norm II, reads: "Infirmi, . . . aliquid sumere possunt . . . per modum potus, vel verae medicinae, exceptis alcoholicis."

[85] Cf. "New Regulations on the Eucharistic Fast," *The Jurist,* XIV (1954), II.

[86] Cf. "Modified discipline of the Eucharistic fast," *Theological Studies,* XIV (1953), 215-241.

[87] Cf. Constitution, n. 31.

It is of no avail to state with Delaney [88] that the exclusion touches alcohol as a drink, not alcohol as a true medicine, for the phrase "*exclusis alcoholicis*" in the Constitution [89] modifies the phrase "*verae medicinae.*" Again, it may be debated whether medical science in modern times ever prescribes alcoholic beverages as a true medicine. Likewise it cannot be asserted that whenever a doctor prescribes it the danger of abuse is thereby averted. While an ounce of brandy or whiskey would not of itself cause mental disturbance to the average individual, nevertheless it might weaken his will power to such an extent that he might take a larger quantity, and thereby render himself unfit for the reception of Holy Communion.

The only real difficulty seems to arise from the question whether a patient may take medicine with an alcoholic base. Hürth states that medicines containing alcohol are excluded completely, but he fails to give a cogent reason for his contention. He gratuitously states that "the Supreme Pontiff did not extend the indult to such alcoholic medicines." [90] This view seems a little too strict when the words of the Instruction [91] are taken into consideration. It states that the sick can take something by way of true medicine, either liquid (exclusive of alcohol) or solid. This can easily be interpreted grammatically to mean "exclusive of alcoholic drinks," which can be more properly understood of alcoholic beverages.[92]

Again, the purpose of the exception is to prevent abuses, and the danger envisioned does not exist in the case of true medicine having a small alcoholic content or alcoholic base. Furthermore, it would be extremely difficult for the average person to determine whether there was any alcohol in a liquid medicine prescribed by a doctor. In this connection many patent medicines have some alcoholic content, which would exclude their

[88] "The new legislation on the Eucharistic fast," *Conference Bulletin of the Archdiocese of New York,* XXXI (1954), 55-73.

[89] Cf. Norm II.

[90] Cf. *op. cit.,* p. 28: ". . . sed Summus Pontifex indultum ad hujusmodi medicinas non extendit."

[91] Cf. n. I.

[92] Cf. Ford, *op. cit.,* pp. 79-80.

use and thus would nullify the law for many persons who would otherwise be entitled to its benefits. In this matter, Conway [93] distinguishes between medicines which contain a minute percentage of alcohol from medicines which contain a considerable proportion thereof. This appears to be an unwarranted distinction, for if it is allowable to take medicine which contains a slight quantity of alcohol, it seems reasonable to be allowed to take it when it contains a considerable proportion, for in neither case is there danger of abuse. Furthermore, one is not likely to err by excess in the taking of such things as medicine.

[93] Cf. *op. cit.*, pp. 43-44.

CHAPTER III

PARTICULAR JURIDICAL NORMS

Article 1. The Sick

Both the decree *Post editum* of 1906 [1] and the Code of Canon Law [2] decreed specifically who were to be included under the heading of sick persons. They included under the heading of sick persons only those who by reason of their sickness were confined to bed for a month without the reasonable hope of a speedy recovery. As soon as the decree was issued commentators questioned the meaning of the word *decumbentes.* They wished to know if a sick person had to be actually bedridden, or if the faculty as granted enabled persons who were simply confined to their homes to benefit by it. Eventually the question was resolved by the Sacred Congregation of the Council on March 6, 1906.[3] The reply stated that the word *decumbentes* included not only those who were habitually confined to their beds, but also those who on account of the nature of their illness could not remain in bed, and those who were able to be up for a few hours each day, provided the doctor thought they could not observe the natural fast.

Anglin [4] believes that since canon 858, § 2, is an authentic interpretation of the decree *Post editum,* the sick person contemplated in this canon includes each and every person included in the phrase "*infirmi qui decumbunt*" of the earlier decree. He maintains that the illness envisioned in canon 858, § 2, must be a grave one, truly considered as such by a physician, or at least considered grave in the common estimation of men.[5]

[1] *Fontes,* n. 4331.

[2] Can. 858, § 2.

[3] Cf. *ASS,* XL (1907), 344; also Anglin, p. 120.

[4] *The Eucharistic Fast,* pp. 121-2.

[5] Cf. *op. cit.,* p. 124.

There now arises the question whether any of the foregoing laws are of any benefit in the interpretation of the word *infirmus* in the present legislation. It does not seem so, for the Constitution states that "the sick, even though not confined to bed, with the prudent advice of a confessor, can take something by way of drink, or of true medicine, excepting alcoholic beverages."[6] Therefore, the law itself states that the question of being confined to bed has nothing whatsoever to do with the interpretation of the word *infirmus.* The Latin word *infirmus* is best translated with the English infirm, since it has a wider meaning than either the words *sick* or *ill,* and it seems that the legislator deliberately chose this word rather than *aegrotus,* which has a much narrower connotation. Thus it may be stated at the outset that the illness here adverted to is not of as serious a character as that which receives mention in the Code of Canon Law.[7]

Moreover, inasmuch as the faculty abstracts from the use of the word *decumbentes,* the implication is that the present law in using the word *infirmus* employs a more extensive term. Furthermore, the law entitles priests, when they are going to say Mass, to make use of the same faculty, which seems to indicate that a grave sickness is not required, for priests when seriously ill are not wont to say Mass during such an illness. Secondly, it can be definitely stated that the advice or the opinion of a doctor is not necessary, though the fact that a person is under a doctor's care may be an indication that he can make use of the faculty, provided, of course, that the resultant subjective inconvenience is also present. Ford[8] gives certain criteria that may be of advantage in one's determining whether or not a given person is a fit subject for the faculty. The fact that a person's lack of good health interferes with his daily duties, or the fact that his friends or neighbors refer to him as a sick person, or the fact that frequently he has to take medicine would be indications at least that he is a fit subject for the privilege. There is practical unanimity among the commentators in stating

[6] Cf. n. 25, Norm II

[7] Can. 858, § 2.

[8] *Op. cit.*, p. 74.

that even temporary infirmities, such as those arising from a severe headache, suffice.[9] It therefore seems that it can be stated as a general principle that, if the person so afflicted would omit Communion because of the requisite fast from midnight, then such a person would find the fast too difficult and could safely be authorized to use the faculty.

While pregnancy is not of itself an illness, nevertheless the state of pregnancy is often accompanied with sickness, and if fasting for such mothers would cause real inconvenience, they too can make use of the privilege.[10] Most of the authors admit that old age is of itself an infirmity,[11] and this view is upheld by the general law of the Code.[12] Ford [13] believes that old age begins at the end of the fifty-ninth year of life in view of the law as it regulates the penitential fast.[14] Conway [15] states that there is a strong presumption that persons over seventy years of age could be regarded as infirm. Undoubtedly, persons who have reached old age may experience more difficulty in observing the Eucharistic fast than they experienced in earlier life, but no definite rule can be set down. In this regard some older persons may be more robust than the younger generation, and, on the other hand, they may also be more reluctant to make use of the concessions. It does not seem that old age of itself has anything whatsoever to do with this matter, though the weakness and frailty resulting therefrom may be a real infirmity. Each case of those who have reached old age must be weighed by the confessor to find out if there is a real inconvenience in the observing of the fast. Unless such a real subjective inconvenience is present, old persons must observe the general law of

9 Cf. Werts, p. 306; Reed, p. 219; Conway, p. 34; Ford, p. 74.

10 Conway, p. 35; Ford, p. 74.

11 Bride, p. 203; Conway, p. 35; Ford, p. 75.

12 Canon 940, § 1: Extrema Unctio praeberi non potest nisi fideli, qui post adeptum usum rationis ob infirmitatem vel senium in periculo mortis versetur.

13 *The New Eucharistic Legislation,* p. 75.

14 Can. 1254, § 2: Lege ieiunii adstringuntur omnes ab expleto vicesimo primo aetatis anno ad inceptum sexagesimum.

15 *The New Law on the Eucharistic Fast,* p. 35.

fasting from all food, drink and medicine, with the exception of water. In this regard it should be remembered that, when the fast is no more difficult than it is for a younger healthy person, the law is the same for all.

Werts[16] reads into the Instruction[17] a distinction between the difficulty experienced by the sick who require liquid food and those who require merely medicine. He states that there are two clauses, one concerning liquids, which are permitted under the condition that fasting is difficult; the other, concerning medicine, which is permitted under the sole condition that it is real medicine. Thus, he maintains that a person with a headache, even though it is not severe enough to make fasting difficult, would still be permitted an aspirin tablet before Communion because he is sick, for aspirin is real medicine.

This seems an unwarranted distinction, and one not intended by the legislator. In the first place the Constitution[18] states that the sick may take something by way of drink or of true medicine, making no distinction between medicine and liquid food. Secondly, the passages referred to in the Instruction are not to be taken disjunctively, as if they connoted two independent privileges. Rather, they are to be taken as one complete statement. The second part is, as it were, governed by the foregoing one. The second part should be read somewhat like this: If the faithful who are sick, even though they are not confined to bed, are by reason of their sickness unable without serious inconvenience to observe the complete fast until the reception of Holy Communion, they can also take something by way of medicine.

Again, authors are unanimous in stating that it is not necessary to wait for the infirmity to develop to such an extent that the person in question could be classified as sick. If a person realizes that a severe headache is developing, and knows from past experience that unless he takes an aspirin tablet he will have a sleepless night, he is entitled to take the tablet, provided he consults the confessor before he receives Holy Communion.

16 "The Eucharistic Fast," *Review for Religious,* XII (1953), 306.

17 Cf. n. I.

18 Cf. n. 25, Norm II.

Such a person could be said to be sick, and it would be a *grave incommodum* for him to refrain from taking the remedies at once.

Ford [19] believes that a person who is the guilty cause of his own sickness, for example, because of over-eating or over-drinking, is not necessarily excluded from the use of the concession, even though he foresaw the necessity of invoking the privilege. At first sight this view seems compatible with the letter of the law inasmuch as such a person could be said to be sick in the meaning of the law. However, if one considers the warning issued to the bishops in the Constitution,[20] namely, "that all irreverence should be guarded against," and "that only those who are in necessity may enjoy these concessions according to the measure of that necessity," [21] this view cannot be sustained. If it is not contrary to the letter of the law, it certainly is not in accord with the spirit thereof. Furthermore, it is difficult to see how such a person could have the requisite dispositions of body and soul for the reception of Holy Communion or for the celebration of Mass. Moreover, the Holy Father stated [22] that those who make use of the faculties should with interior penance, or with some other means in accordance with the traditional custom of the Church, make up for the lessened discomfort of the body. If persons who through no fault of their own are expected to do these things, then, surely, the person who is the willing cause of his own sickness should not be allowed to benefit by the new concessions.

Article 2. The Necessary Conditions That Must be Present

The fact that a person is sick within the meaning of the term *infirmus* as used in the Constitution does not *ipso facto* entitle him to the benefits of the new legislation. Other conditions must also be present, namely, there must be (a) a serious subjective inconvenience, (b) arising from the infirmity, and (c)

[19] *The New Eucharistic Legislation,* p. 75.

[20] Cf. n. 31.

[21] Cf. n. 9.

[22] Cf. Constitution, n. 31.

the presence of these conditions must be weighed by the confessor, who is entitled to give the required advice. All the listed conditions must be verified at one and the same time.

It should be noted, first of all, that there is always a certain inconvenience felt in observing the Eucharistic fast, an inconvenience experienced by those in robust health as well as by those who are ill. Such inconvenience is not meant in the present context, and the fact that the sick experience only such an inconvenience does not entitle them to apply for the privilege. The legislator is here referring to a serious subjective inconvenience, which arises not from the fast as such, but rather from the fact that the person is sick and therefore fasting causes him some serious inconvenience. Thus, if a sick person, regardless of the gravity of his illness, experiences no greater inconvenience in observing the fast than he felt when he was in good health, or only an inconvenience that can be alleviated with the drinking of a glass of water, such a person is still bound to observe the Eucharistic fast. This is in conformity with the statement in the Instruction [23] that the faithful who are sick can take something by way of drink, if by reason of their sickness they are unable to observe the complete fast. Furthermore, even though a sick person experiences some serious subjective inconvenience as arising from the sickness, he is not thereby entitled to the reception of Holy Communion when he has broken the fast, until he has sought and received the advice of the confessor. This advice is never to be presumed.

In this regard it may be stated that it is not necessary to seek the advice every time one wishes to go to Communion. As Conway remarks,[24] the confessor gives his judgment on a particular situation, and this judgment remains valid as long as the circumstances are not substantially changed. Thus a pregnant mother, if she experiences a serious inconvenience as arising from the sickness accompanying her pregnancy may seek the advice once, and such advice suffices as long as her condition makes the observance of the fast seriously inconvenient. Similarly a convalescing person need seek the advice only once for

[23] Cf. n. I.

[24] *The New Law on the Eucharistic Fast,* p. 37.

the whole period of his convalescence. In other words, the advice may be given "*semel pro semper*" when there is question of a continuing or recurrent infirmity that causes the serious inconvenience. As is stated in the Instruction,[25] the advice may be given once and for all as long as the conditions of the same sickness continue to exist.

There is no unanimity among canonists on whether the above stated rules bind the clergy as well as the laity. In other words, is it necessary that the serious subjective inconvenience be present in every case, and must the advice of the confessor be sought by priests as well as by the faithful? In this matter the wording of the Instruction[26] differs somewhat from the Constitution.[27] The Constitution implies that the faculty is granted only to priests who are about to celebrate Mass, but the Instruction clarifies the matter and states that they can enjoy the faculty whether they are going to celebrate or simply will receive after the manner of the laity. But neither the Constitution nor the Instruction makes it clear whether the grave inconvenience must be present or not, or whether priests also must consult a confessor.

Ford[28] believes that priests enjoy this faculty only under the same conditions as the laity, though he admits that the contrary opinion is also probable. He bases his view on the wording of the law. He translates the word "*pariter*" to mean "in like manner", so that priests can use the faculty only when the same conditions are present that are demanded for the laity. But the word "*pariter*" does not necessarily mean "in like manner." Rather, it seems that it should be translated as "also." The text would then read as follows: Priests who are ill, even if they are not confined to bed, may also avail them-

[25] Cf. n. 2.

[26] N. 3.—Sacerdotes infirmi, etiamsi non decumbant, dispensatione pariter uti possunt, sive sint Missam celebraturi, sive Sanctissimam Eucharistiam recepturi.

[27] N. 25, Norm II.—Eadem facultas sacerdotibus infirmis conceditur Missam celebraturis.

[28] *The New Eucharistic Legislation*, pp. 80-82.

selves of the dispensation, whether they are going to celebrate Mass or receive the Most Holy Eucharist.[29]

Secondly, priests who are empowered by law to dispense the faithful from the obligation of the law of fast and abstinence may use the faculty in their own favor.[30] In the same way priests who are entitled to give the advice to others can make the required decision in their own cases. Again, the Constitution in Norm III, which deals specifically with the law for priests, does not demand the advice of the confessor, though Norm V demands both inconvenience and the advice of the confessor in the case of the faithful. Furthermore, the precise reason why the advice is needed in the case of the faithful is to make sure that the postulated subjective inconvenience is present, but the priest who does this for others should be capable of doing so for himself also. Again, in other passages the word "faithful" is used in contradistinction to the word "priests." In the Instruction[31] the explicit statement that the faithful must seek a confessor's advice before they receive Communion implies at least that such advice is not necessary in the case of priests. Finally, it would be extremely difficult for priests in mission territory to seek the advice of a priest, and yet it was such priests in particular who were given consideration by the legislator in his granting of the faculty.[32]

It must be admitted, however, that it is not clear, either from the Constitution[33] or from the Instruction,[34] that a subjective inconvenience is required on the part of the sick priests before they can make use of the concessions. However, the fact that in the Constitution[35] the Supreme Pontiff emphasized that the

[29] This is the rendering given by Conway, *op. cit.*, p. 21; also by Bouscaren, *The Canon Law Digest*, Supplement under canon 808.

[30] Can. 1245, § 1.

[31] Cf. n. 11: " . neque absque eiusdem consilio fideles non ieiuni sanctissimam Eucharistiam recipere possunt."

[32] Cf. Constitution, n. 13.

[33] Cf. n. 25. Norm II.

[34] Cf. n. 3.

[35] Cf. n. 9.

law of the Eucharistic fast is to be retained in full force (water excepted), and that those who are able to obey this law would do so, so that only those who are in necessity may enjoy the concessions, is a clear indication that priests also must be subject to a real inconvenience before they can avail themselves of the privilege. This view is corroborated in a private reply of the Holy Office of January 28, 1953. The response stated that priests who have a physical condition so robust as not to feel a serious inconvenience from fasting cannot avail themselves of the concessions made by the Holy Father in the Apostolic Constitution *Christus Dominus.*[36]

Article 3. The Food, Drink and Medicine Allowed

Since the law[37] states that the sick can take something *per modum potus* before Communion, all solid foods are thereby excluded. Not only that, but also those foods which cannot be regarded as either liquids or solids in the strict meaning of the terms remain excluded. Thus, foods which cannot be classified as either liquids or solids are here to be regarded as solids and thereby are excluded. Alcoholic drinks, even when prescribed as medicine by a doctor are also excluded. This is true, even when these drinks are taken in milk, coffee or some other liquid, as long as the resultant beverage is regarded as an alcoholic drink. Again, there is no limit on the amount of liquid food taken or on the number of times it is taken.

The only requirement in the law regarding medicine is that it be true medicine, whether prescribed by a doctor or commonly regarded by people as such. As long as it fulfills the notion of a curative, palliative or preventive measure in regard to sickness it can be regarded as a medicine. Moreover, it can be taken in either liquid or solid form.[38] Furthermore, the law places no limit on the amount taken, nor on the number of times it is taken. In this matter, however, there is little danger of abuse, as people are not likely to err by excess in the taking of medicine. Again the sick, whether priests or laity, may avail

[36] Cf. Bouscaren, *The Canon Law Digest,* Supplement under canon 808.

[37] Cf. Constitution, n. 25; Instruction, n. 2.

[38] Cf. Instruction, n. I.

themselves of the concession whether the Mass be celebrated or Holy Communion be received in the morning or in the evening.

ARTICLE 4. THE TIME WHEN SUCH FOOD AND MEDICINE ARE ALLOWED

From an examination of the Constitution alone, one would have difficulty in determining if there was a time limit placed on the sick, whether priests or laity, who wish to benefit by this concession. At first sight it could seem that an hour should have elapsed after the consumption of liquids or medicine before the reception of Holy Communion, as is set down for those in special circumstances in Norms III and IV. Such is not the case, however, for the Instruction[39] states that in the case of the sick no duration of elapsed time needs to be present between the taking of the required drink or medicine and the reception of Holy Communion. Thus the laity, or also sick priests who receive Communion after the manner of the laity, may take liquids or true medicine without respect to any lapse of time before Communion. Sick priests about to celebrate Mass can avail themselves of the faculty up to the very moment when Mass begins. In other words, the sick, whether priests or laity, may avail themselves of this privilege just as they can avail themselves of the privilege of taking water, provided of course that the other required conditions are present.

It may here be noted that the new legislation omits altogether any mention of religious. Consequently, religious, whether women or men, unless the latter are ordained priests, must in this matter follow the rules set down for the faithful in general.

[39] Cf. n. 2.

CHAPTER IV

THE EUCHARISTIC FAST FOR PRIESTS

Article 1. Priests Who Must Celebrate at a Late Hour

The Apostolic Constitution [1] gives to priests who are going to celebrate either at a late hour, or after onerous work in the sacred ministry, or after a long journey, the faculty of taking liquid food, exclusive of alcoholic drinks, up to one hour before the beginning of Mass. This is a completely new privilege without precedent in either the Code or the pre-Code law.

It has already been shown that priests who are ill cannot avail themselves of the granted faculties unless the fasting cause them serious inconvenience. The same argument can be used in reference to the present privilege to show that the inconvenience must also be present before this faculty can be utilized. This inconvenience must be one arising not from the Eucharistic fast as such, but rather because of the fasting to a late hour. In considering the present faculty, therefore, one must first decide what is the meaning of the phrase *tardioribus horis*. The Constitution itself gives no indication of how this is to be understood, but the Instruction [2] interprets it to mean a Mass beginning after nine o'clock. In reckoning the hour of nine o'clock one may make use of any of the various manners of computation specified in the Code.[3] Thus, a priest or a layman in using the present faculty uses the same method of reckoning nine o'clock as he uses in computing midnight.

1 Cf. n. 26, Norm III.

2 Cf. n. 4.

3 Can. 33, § 1.—In reckoning the hours of the day, the common local usage is to be followed; but for the private celebration of Holy Mass, the private recitation of the Divine Office, the reception of Holy Communion, and the observance of fast and abstinence, even though the usual local computation of time be a divergent one, one may follow the local time, true or mean, or the legal time, regional or extraordinary.

Is nine o'clock to be taken as a late hour for the universal Church, or is it merely given as a norm for particular areas? Coronata [4] believes the hour of nine o'clock is mentioned because in Italy the working-day begins between six and seven o'clock in the morning, and persons who are out of bed for from two to three hours would regard nine o'clock as a late hour. But since different customs prevail in different regions, nine o'clock cannot be regarded universally as a late hour. Consequently, he believes the local ecclesiastical authority should specify the corresponding late hour in his own particular territory after having taken into consideration the customs of the place concerning the beginning of the working day, the time of rising, etc., or, in default of this, the confessor is to decide. There does not seem to be any foundation for this opinion which, if put into practice, would beget a multitude of anxieties and scruples on the part of the faithful, as well as a multitude of customs which the legislator expressly intended to obviate.[5]

Is the hour of nine o'clock to be reckoned physically or morally? Just as midnight is to be reckoned physically, so the computation of nine o'clock is to be reckoned physically also. According to the more common opinion of canonists midnight begins at the first stroke of the clock, so in the present legislation nine o'clock begins at the first stroke.[6] Thus a priest who begins Mass immediately after the first stroke of nine o'clock can be said to be saying Mass after nine, and such a priest is entitled to use the privilege if the other condition, namely a subjective inconvenience, is present.[7] Since the time is to be computed mathematically, a complete hour of abstinence from everything except water must have elapsed before the beginning of Mass. Thus, if a priest who is scheduled to say the nine o'clock Mass realizes that he took liquids even one minute after eight o'clock,

[4] *De Nova Disciplina Ieiunii Eucharistici,* p. 79.

[5] Cf. Constitution, n. 22.

[6] Cf. Anglin, p. 91.

[7] Ford (p. 86) states that a Mass scheduled for nine o'clock, even if begun promptly, will not actually begin until after nine o'clock because of the time it takes to proceed to the altar, etc. Mass begins when the priest says "*In nomine Patris*" at the foot of the altar.

he is not permitted to begin Mass until the hour has elapsed. Just as all moral approximation of midnight is forbidden, so in the present legislation the hour must be computed physically, and a priest who knowingly would begin Mass before the physical lapse of an hour would sin gravely.

Commentators are not in agreement on whether there must be a reasonable cause for saying Mass at a late hour before the concession can be used. Onclin[8] believes that the late hour may be freely selected so that a person who deliberately stays up late the previous night and takes a long sleep in the morning can avail himself of the privilege. Connell[9] and Conway[10] maintain that the priest who conscientously believes he needs a long sleep on a particular morning can use the concession. These opinions, though they may appear in harmony with the letter of the law, cannot be sustained for the following reasons. In the first place, the serious inconvenience must be always present, and according to the mind of the legislator it must arise from the fact that the priest is obliged to say Mass at a late hour. In the case in question there is no obligation to celebrate at a late hour. The hour is deliberately selected, so that the person may avail himself of the privilege, which is not in keeping with the statement "that only those in necessity may enjoy the concessions according to the measure of that necessity."[11]

Secondly, the legislator had not such cases in mind when he instituted the law; rather, he was considering those priests who had to say Mass at a late hour because of the missionary nature of their work, or because of the necessity of providing Mass for the faithful in large industrial centers where people could not assist at an earlier one.[12] Furthermore the Holy Father forbade

8 "La nouvelle legislation sur le jeûne ecclesiastique," *Ephemerides Theologicae Lovanienses*, XXIX (1953), 91.

9 "The New Rules for the Eucharistic Fast," *AER*, CXXVIII (1953), 249.

10 *The New Law on the Eucharistic Fast*, p. 48.

11 Constitution, n. 9.

12 Cf. Constitution, n. 12, where the Pope speaks of overburdened priests because of the nature of their work, etc.

any amplification of the faculties.[13] But to include such cases as this is certainly extending the faculties beyond the meaning of the words, which is precisely what the legislator forbade.

Another problem agitating the minds of commentators in this matter is the question of a priest who celebrates two or three Masses the same day and for whom fasting is seriously inconvenient. Can such a priest take the permitted liquids both before the earlier Massas as well as before the Mass celebrated by him after nine o'clock. Unless such a priest is allowed to take liquids before the first, in most cases he will not be permitted to avail himself of the privilege at all, because of the close proximity of the second and third Mass to the first one. For example, a priest who celebrates Mass at eight, nine and ten o'clock would not be allowed to take liquids between them because the required hour would not have elapsed and thus the purpose of the law would be frustrated. Again, the law merely demands a late Mass or a Mass after nine o'clock, and says nothing of earlier ones. Thus a priest who says an earlier one also is still within the law because he fulfills the notion of saying a late Mass. As long as he takes no liquids for the duration of one hour before one late Mass, or before each of several Masses when one of these is celebrated after nine o'clock, he is within the meaning of the law.[14]

Another question related to the foregoing is that of a priest who is scheduled to say a late Mass on Sunday and who has taken liquid food after midnight. Can such a practice be reconciled with the faculty in question? It seems that this procedure can be permitted if it can be prudently foreseen that the

[13] Cf. Constitution, n. 13.

[14] Cf. Hürth, p. 33; also Castellano, "Ad novam disciplinam circa ieiunium eucharisticum commentarium," *Monitor Ecclesiasticus,* LXXVIII (1953), 407, where he states: "Concessio sacerdotibus, qui in adiunctis a lege probatis versantur, facta aliquid sumendi per modum potus 'servato ieiunio unius horae ante Missae celebrationem,' sic intelligenda est ut ipsi aliquid per modum potus sumere permittantur ante quamlibet Missam, ideoque, si bis vel ter celebrant, tum ante primam, tum ante secundam, tum ante tertiam, *dummodo hoc fiat una saltem hora ante unamquamque Missam.*"

required serious inconvenience arising from fasting till a late hour will be present. If, for example, a priest is morally certain from past experience that he will suffer a severe headache unless he has some liquid food, there does not seem to be anything in the law to prohibit him from taking liquids in the early hours of the morning.

Article. 2. Priests Who Celebrate After Onerous Work in the Sacred Ministry

The second reason why priests may take liquid food when the fasting causes serious inconvenience is their onerous work in the sacred ministry.[15] This faculty is explained somewhat in the Instruction,[16] where an example of onerous work is given as work from early morning or for a long period of time. This example is helpful in understanding the concession, for it implies that the work here referred to must be grave either by reason of its duration or by reason of its intensity. In this matter it should be remembered that it is work in the sacred ministry, that is to say, work which has for its primary end and purpose the salvation of souls. Such work would include the administration of the sacraments, assisting at or performing sacred functions, preaching, catechizing, and whatever work can be said to be the work of the priest rather than the work of the faithful.

Ford [17] believes that a priest who works all night preparing a manuscript in order to meet a deadline would qualify under this heading. It would be difficult to visualise how this type of work could be interpreted as having any relationship with ministerial work. The law postulates that it be work in the sacred ministry, and this should be interpreted according to the proper meaning of the words. This, however, is not merely a liberal interpretation of the text; it is also an extensive one and as such must be rejected. Likewise a priest who stays up with a sick person all night cannot take advantage of the privilege, for this is not work of the sacred ministry as such, but rather a work of charity. However, such a priest might be entitled to break the Eucharis-

[15] Constitution, n. 26, Norm IV.

[16] Cf. n. 4 (b).

[17] *The New Eucharistic Legislation,* p. 87.

tic fast under the privilege granted to the faithful under the title of exhausting labor.[18] On the other hand, a priest who in the morning spent some time in preparing a sermon would qualify, for such work could be regarded as work in the sacred ministry.

It is difficult to make a correct judgment of the meaning of " a long period of time " or " from early morning." Castellano [19] believes that it would require two hours in the hearing of confessions for a young healthy priest to qualify. In this regard it seems as if a distinction should be made between hard work in the ministry *ratione temporis* and hard work *ratione intensitatis.* In no case could thirty minutes be regarded as hard work *ratione temporis,* but thirty minutes spent in the hearing of confessions could be regarded as hard work *ratione intensitatis.* The same would be true of a priest who preaches a twenty minute sermon at an earlier Mass. It seems, however, that in this matter no definite period of time can be set down as a minimum. Again, it must be remembered that a relative norm rather than an absolute one must be used, for while an hour's work may fatigue one person it may cause no serious inconvenience to another. It could be stated as a general rule, however, that work in the sacred ministry for one hour *ratione temporis* or for thirty minutes *ratione intensitatis* would fulfill what is postulated for this concession. However, the circumstances of each case must be prudently weighed; whatever amount of work either by reason of its duration or intensity causes serious subjective inconvenience entitles one to use the concession. But as in all other cases, the inconvenience must be something arising from the work in the ministry *ratione durationis* or *ratione intensitatis,* and not from the fast as such.

It might be debated whether a priest who is engaged in onerous ministerial work on Saturday can use this privilege on Sunday morning. It frequently happens that on important feast days such as Christmas and Easter a priest in a large city parish may hear confessions for several hours on the previous day and often late into the night. Can such a priest use the faculty on

[18] Cf. Constitution, n. 28, Norm V; Instruction, n. 10 a.

[19] Cf. " art. cit.," *Monitor Ecclesiasticus,* LXXIX (1954), 30.

the following day? It does not seem so, since there is no real connection between the work of the previous day and the fast for Mass. The very fact that work from early morning is mentioned as a requirement for the use of the concession seems to exclude completely the work of the previous day. However, if the work that was begun on Saturday is carried on into the early hours of Sunday morning, the use of the concession appears warranted. Again, a priest who foresees on rising that he will have to engage in onerous work in the ministry which he knows from past experience will cause serious inconvenience may take the permitted liquids before the work begins.

Article 3. Priests Who Celebrate After a Long Journey

The long journey mentioned in the Constitution[20] is interpreted by the Instruction[21] as a journey on foot of two kilometers (about a mile and a quarter), or proportionately longer according to the type of vehicle used, as long as there is due consideration also of the difficulty of the journey or of the particular person making the journey. The first question one should resolve in interpreting this faculty is to ascertain whether the journey in question must be made for the celebration of Mass.

Conway[22] believes that the journey could be one made for some other motive. He submits by way of example the case of a priest who goes to the other end of the parish to deliver a message. This view, for two reasons, does not seem to be admissible. In the first place, the Instruction speaks of priests who are going to celebrate after a long journey, the implication being that the journey is necessary in order that the priest be able to celebrate Mass. Thus a priest who could celebrate Mass close to his residence would not be justified in going to a church in a distant part of town in order to benefit by the faculty. Similarly a priest could not undertake a long walk for purely physical exercise in order to benefit by this concession. The Mass must be necessary, or, if not, the journey must at least be one that is made for the precise purpose of saying Mass. Thus a

[20] Cf. n. 26, Norm III.

[21] Cf. n. 8 c.

[22] *The New Law on the Eucharistic Fast*, p. 50.

priest who travels this distance to say Mass *causa devotionis* could not use the privilege. Secondly, this opinion is the only one that can be reconciled with the statement in the Constitution,[23] wherein the Holy Father speaks of priests whose duty it is to make a long journey in order that large sections of the faithful may not be deprived of Mass.

Could a priest who has to travel a long journey before Mass to administer the sacraments to a dying person make use of this faculty? It does not seem so, inasmuch as such a journey would not fulfill the notion of travelling the journey in order to say Mass. Nor would it be in keeping with the statement of the Instruction quoted above, which speaks of the journey being made lest the faithful would be deprived of the privilege of assisting at Mass.[24] Such a priest, however, could avail himself of this privilege under another heading, namely, that of a priest who celebrates Mass after onerous work in the sacred ministry, provided of course that the journey caused the serious inconvenience which is always postulated for the warranted use of these faculties. Similarly, a priest who walks a mile and a quarter in order to receive Communion rather than to celebrate Mass could not use this faculty, though again he could benefit under the same privilege which is given to the laity in similar circumstances. It may, therefore, be stated as a general principle that the journey must be made for the precise purpose of saying Mass, whether the Mass is one of obligation or merely of devotion.

There is some disagreement among commentators as to what would constitute a proportionately longer journey according to the type of vehicle used. In this matter, no definite minimum journey can be set down. Several circumstances must be taken into consideration, such as the type of vehicle used, the season of the year, the condition of the roads, the age and health of the priest in question, etc. While a journey of a half-hour for a priest in delicate health might cause serious inconvenience, a much longer journey for a robust priest might cause no inconvenience whatsoever. It may be stated, then, that any journey for which a vehicle is used and which consumes the same amount

[23] Cf. n. 12.

[24] Cf. n. 12.

of time as a journey of a mile and a quarter on foot would be sufficient to permit the priest to use this concession, provided the postulated inconvenience be present. In practice, the minimum amount of requisite time when a vehicle is used appears to be approximately half an hour.

Ford [25] believes it reasonable to suppose that the journey on foot, also, may be considered in the light of the difficulties of both the particular journey and the particular person, and may therefore be less than two kilometers. He bases his view on the words of the Instruction,[26] which he claims are not quite clear. His difficulty is in interpreting whether the last clause in the statement, "post longum iter (i.e. saltem 2 km. circiter pedibus percurrendum, vel proportionate longius pro variis vehiculis adhibitis, *difficultatis quoque itineris vel personae habita ratione*"), refers only to what immediately precedes, or also to the first part of the sentence. It seems that there is nothing in the punctuation or in the construction that shows that the final clause refers only to the case when a vehicle is used. However, the word *saltem* in numbers four and ten of the Instruction seems to fix two kilometers as a strict minimum, not affected by the final clause in the sentence in any way.

Article 4. The Consumption of the Ablutions at the First Mass

The Apostolic Constitution gives to priests who binate or trinate the faculty of taking the ablutions at the earlier Masses.[27] These ablutions, however, must be effected with water alone, which no longer breaks the Eucharistic fast. The Instruction [28] in interpreting this faculty restricts it in two cases. It states that one who celebrates three Masses, one after the other on Christmas Day or on All Souls' Day, is obliged to observe the rubrics with regard to the ablutions. It is important to note here that the law refers to Masses said one after another, implying

[25] *The New Eucharistic Legislation*, p. 88.

[26] Cf. nn. 4 and 10.

[27] Cf. n. 27, Norm IV.

[28] Cf. nn. 7 and 8.

that, when some period of time elapses between the Masses, the ablutions may be taken even on these two days.

Now the law also states that if a priest who has to celebrate Mass twice or three times should inadvertently take wine also in the ablution, he is not forbidden to say the second or third Mass.[29] This statement has been the source of much discussion. Canonists are not in agreement in determining the exact meaning of the phrase "a priest who has to celebrate Mass." What is the precise force of the word *debet*? Does it mean that there is an obligation to celebrate the further Masses?

Conway [30] seems to think that such an obligation must exist. In this view a priest who is celebrating the second or third Mass on Christmas Day or on All Souls' Day *causa devotionis* could not continue if he inadvertently took the ablutions in the first Mass. McCarthy [31] believes that if the Holy Office wished to imply such a necessity or obligation it would surely not have used this neutral word. However, this interpretation is not admissible. The word *debet* must be understood here according to its proper meaning, which implies an obligation on the part of the priest to say the second or third Mass.

Similarly, a priest who has an obligation to say a second Mass in the afternoon cannot intentionally take the ablutions with wine in the morning Mass, even though he is entitled to take wine at the meal that intervenes. However, if he inadvertently takes the wine ablutions at the morning Mass, he can still celebrate in the evening, provided that there is some obligation for saying the evening Mass.[32] The wording of the law must be adhered to in this matter, and the law does not distinguish between Masses celebrated in the morning or in the afternoon.

29 Cf. Instruction, n. 8.—Si vero sacerdos, qui bis vel ter Missam celebrare debet per inadvertentiam vinum quoque in ablutione sumat, non vetatur quominus secundam et tertiam Missam celebret.

30 *The New Law on the Eucharistic Fast*, p. 57.

31 Cf. "Notes and Queries," *The Irish Ecclesiastical Record* (Dublin, 1864-) 5. series, LXXXII (1954), 418-420.

32 Cf. Instruction n. 13.

CHAPTER V

THE EUCHARISTIC FAST FOR THE LAITY

THE new Eucharistic legislation, just as it does in the case of priests, provides special concessions for the laity who, though indeed they are not sick, are placed in such particular circumstances that they are unable to observe the complete Eucharistic fast without serious inconvenience. The law demands in the case of the laity, as also it does in the case of priests about to celebrate Mass, a serious subjective inconvenience which must arise from one or another of the three sets of circumstances mentioned, namely, (a) the exhausting labor undertaken before the reception of Holy Communion; (b) the rather late hour when Holy Communion is received, and (c) the long journey travelled for reaching the church. It furthermore requires that, before the reception of Holy Communion, the subject must submit his case to a confessor, who then makes a prudent judgment on the facts as presented in order to decide if all the requirements are present. This last requirement, as already shown, does not obtain in the case of priests, for they are not required to make any such consultation.

Both priests and laity on the fulfillment of the above stated requirements are allowed to take liquid food, but they must abstain from all alcoholic beverages from the previous midnight. There is one other difference between these very similar faculties that should be noted, namely, while the priest must abstain from all liquid food for one complete hour before the beginning of Mass, the laity need abstain for an hour simply before the reception of Holy Communion.[1]

The three causes which are presumed to give rise to the serious inconvenience will be treated separately in the following articles.

[1] Apostolic Constitution, n. 28, Norm V; Instruction, n. 9.

Article 1. The Laity Engaged in Exhausting Labor

Though the Constitution and the Instruction speak of exhausting labor as one of the causes which gives rise to the serious inconvenience, and though the Instruction in addition gives examples of what constitutes it, nevertheless, nowhere in the law is it defined. However, it may be stated at the outset that in determining the notion of exhausting labor one need not rely on a scientific evaluation. Like the question of grave inconvenience, and the notion of liquids, the criterion one is to use in determining it is the common estimation of men.

The law gives no indication whether the work here envisioned is physical labor, or mental labor, or a combination of both. While the examples given in the Instruction [2] all refer to physical work or to labor that concerns the use of the body rather than that of the mind, nevertheless it should be remembered that an exhaustive list is not there indicated. The use of the phrases *et cetera* and *verbi gratia* at the end of the list indicate that it is merely a demonstrative one. Again, the listing of causes which by way of example derive from physical work does not exclude the causes that derive from mental labor. Furthermore, it is common knowledge that mental labor can be equally as exhausting as physical labor, especially when engaged in for a notable period of time. Thus it seems that students, teachers, lawyers, authors and all those whose work is of a mental rather than of a physical nature can use this faculty if and when the other required suppositions are present. Furthermore, it should be stated here that the work, whether physical or mental, must be of such a nature as to cause notable fatigue, and that this fatigue can be removed only through the consumption of some food. Thus a very slight feeling of tiredness or weariness arising from work would not fulfill the notion of exhausting labor.

The Instruction [3] treats of three different categories of persons whose work is of such a nature that it could be described as exhausting. To the first category belong all those who are habitually engaged in night work in public utility services,

[2] Cf. n. 10a.

[3] Cf. n. 10a.

such as factory workers, dock workers, railroad employees, police, soldiers, sailors, post office workers, telephone and telegraph operators, etc. In a word, this category includes all those who are employed by the state or local government, if their work is so connected with the public good of the state or local community that the national economy or the good of that community would suffer were their work curtailed or completely omitted. All such people who habitually work day and night shifts are included in this category and may benefit by the concessions of the law whenever the requisite conditions are fulfilled.

It may be difficult at times to decide whether some such persons are really night workers, inasmuch as they go to work in the early hours of the morning rather than that they work at night. No definite rule can be set down, and accordingly the matter must be judged in the light of the common estimation of men and in line with the local customs. In practice it seems to matter little, for it will be shown that those who go to work in the early hours of the morning can benefit by the law as well as those who work through the night. It can be stated, however, that persons employed in public utility works, if they work through the greater part of the night, for example, if they work from four o'clock in the afternoon till midnight, or from eight o'clock in the evening to four in the morning, or from midnight to eight o'clock in the morning, or in general those who work during the hours of darkness rather than during the hours of daylight, are generally regarded as night workers. In doubt whether a particular person could be classified as a night worker the confessor should decide in the subject's favor.

To the second category belong those who by reason of their office or by reason of charity work during the night. Among such people are doctors, nurses, night watchmen, hotel clerks, cab drivers, printers, radio and television announcers, entertainers, etc. In a word this category includes all those who, though not engaged in works of public utility, earn their livelihood by working at night at least for a part of the time. It should be noted here that the law includes night workers who work out of charity as well as those who work out of necessity.

Again, it is not necessary that their charitable works be habitual ones. They can avail themselves of the concessions even though they work at night only by way of special occasion (*per modum actus*). Thus a person who stays up one night to care for a sick relative or friend, or a person who stays up for an hour in nocturnal adoration of the Blessed Sacrament, would qualify because this is a work of charity.

Conway[4] includes in this category farmers, hotel servants, agricultural workers and all those who go to work in the early hours of the morning. While such persons may be engaged in exhausting labor and thus become entitled to the use of this faculty, nevertheless they are so entitled not because of the fact that they can be regarded as night workers, but rather because they spend a considerable period of time in exhausting labor in the morning before they can receive Holy Communion.

The third and final category of persons engaged in exhausting labor as mentioned in the Instruction includes those who work for a long time before Communion. In this category two examples are given, namely, pregnant women and mothers of families. There is some dispute as to the proper interpretation of this sentence.[5] The wording of the law seems somewhat ambiguous. It is not clear whether the phrase "*quae per longum tempus incumbere debent*" refers solely to "*matresfamilias*" or also to "*mulieres praegnantes.*" Hürth[6] believes that it refers solely to "*matresfamilias,*" so that pregnancy of itself would entitle one to the use of this concession. He bases his opinion on the fact that the Holy See has been wont to grant this faculty to pregnant women in the past. However, as the statement stands, it seems that the clause "*quae per longum tempus incumbere debent*" refers to both "*matresfamilias*" and to "*mulieres praegnantes.*" In other words, pregnant women who have no household duties to perform may not avail themselves of the faculty under this heading. In this regard it should be noted

[4] *The New Law on the Eucharistic Fast,* p. 50.

[5] ". . . tum mulieres praegnantes et matresfamilias quae, antequam ecclesiam adire queant, in domesticis negotiis per longum tempus incumbere debent."

[6] *De Nova Disciplina Ieiunii Eucharistici,* p. 38.

that pregnancy is in itself (*per se*) a normal natural state for a woman, so that what is natural and normal should not of itself prove so difficult as to cause serious inconvenience in the matter of fasting for a short period of time. However, inasmuch as pregnancy is often accompanied with sickness, such cases are already provided for through another concession in this law,[7] so that pregnant mothers who are habitually ill can have liquid food or medicine before Communion.

Another difficulty in this matter rests in the determining of the period of time that would constitute a long time. The Instruction gives some indication, for it simply refers to mothers of families who must engage in household tasks for a long time before they receive Communion. With modern facilities a mother could without too much difficulty prepare breakfast for her husband and get one, two or three children prepared for school or church in an hour. This normally would be the only work required of a mother before Mass, so it seems that a mother who does such house work for an hour before Mass would be entitled to use this privilege. Those who have to do much lighter work, such as watching a sick person, must look to a correspondingly longer period of time, but it is generally agreed among commentators that two hours of any work could be regarded as fulfilling this requirement.[8] However, it should be remembered that the work must be necessary, whether done out of charity or out of strict duty. One could not undertake the work simply to avail oneself of the faculty. The only test therefore for the confessor to apply is this: has this person to do this work either during the night or in the early hours of the morning, so that it is seriously inconvenient to fast until after Communion?

Article 2. The Laity Who Receive Communion at a Late Hour

The Apostolic Constitution or also the accompanying Instruction does not state explicitly the precise meaning of the "late hour" for the laity. Nor does either of these state whether the late hour is to be considered relatively or absolutely. However,

[7] Cf. Apostolic Constitution, n. 25, Norm II; Instruction, n. I.

[8] Cf. Conway, *The New Law on the Eucharistic Fast,* p. 51.

the fact that the Instruction [9] states that nine o'clock is an absolutely late hour for priests who are going to celebrate Mass is a definite indication that the same can be regarded as a late hour for the laity also. Thus it may be stated at the outset that a lay person who fulfills the other necessary requirements and who is going to receive Communion after nine o'clock may take advantage of this concession.

But the late hour can be considered in a relative sense. This is clear from the Constitution,[10] where the Supreme Pontiff speaks of the difficulty encountered by children who wish to receive Communion on weekdays and who have to return home for breakfast before proceeding to school. If the law were to postulate nine o'clock as the absolute late hour, such children could never benefit by the concessions, for in all countries children have to be in school by nine o'clock. Indeed, the purpose of the law was to benefit such children, but in consequence of the demand of an absolute standard the purpose of the law would be frustrated. The same would be true of various classes of people whose work is of such a nature that it prevents them from attending an early Mass, and yet it was intended that these too should benefit from this legislation. Thus a workman who goes to an eight o'clock Mass and then proceeds to work is entitled to the use of the faculty whenever it would be difficult for him to return home for breakfast before his working day begins. On the other hand, such workmen who can return home for breakfast without serious inconvenience cannot rightfully feel entitled to the use of the faculty. In other words, they must have a serious reason for going to the late Mass, whether the late hour is an absolute or a relative one. Again, a person who is habitually entitled to the use of the concession cannot do so on an occasion when he can easily attend an earlier Mass.[11]

There has been much discussion among canonists regarding the kind of necessity that must underlie one's act of selecting attendance at a late Mass if one is rightfully to benefit from this concession. That some necessity is required for the faithful

[9] Cf. n. 4.

[10] Cf. n. 17.

[11] Cf. Hürth, *De Nova Disciplina Ieiunii Eucharistici*, pp. 39, 40.

seems to be evident from the text of the Constitution: "Christifideles . . . qui ob grave incommodum omnino ieiuni adire nequeant, . . . hac perdurante necessitate, aliquid sumere possunt. . . ." [12] Furthermore, earlier in the decree it is established as a general principle that only those who are under necessity can benefit from the concessions according to the measure of that necessity.[13] Must it be absolutely impossible to get to an earlier Mass, or is a serious inconvenience in getting to an earlier one sufficient? The general consensus seems to be that any reasonable cause suffices in one's selecting attendance at a later Mass.

Hürth [14] states that any real necessity suffices. He cites as a real necessity the case of a person who wishes to receive Communion with the other members of a Sodality or pious association at a late Mass, though he could have received at an earlier one. He believes that it would be a real inconvenience for such a person to go to an earlier Mass, return home for breakfast, and then return to the church to join his group at a later Mass. In the same way an altar boy who is assigned to serve at a late Mass has a title to the use of the faculty, even though he could have received Communion at an earlier mass.[15]

Some canonists believe that a person who inadvertently takes some liquids after midnight can select a late Mass for the reception of Holy Communion.[16] They seem to base their opinions on the fact that the persons in question do not set the hour in order to drink, but set it in order to receive Communion. Furthermore, they state that there is a reasonable cause for selecting that late hour. This opinion cannot be reconciled with the wording of the law which speaks of those "who can draw near the Holy Banquet *only* at a rather late hour," which implies some real inconvenience that prevents them from assisting at an earlier Mass. Nor is it in keeping with the purpose of the law,

[12] Cf. n. 28, Norm V.

[13] Cf. Apostolic Constitution, n. 9.

[14] Cf. *op. cit.*, p. 40.

[15] Cf. Connell, "The New Rules for the Eucharistic Fast," *AER*, CXXVIII (1953), 251.

[16] Reed, "Select Questions on the Eucharistic Fast," *Theological Studies*. XVI (1955), 53; also Connell, "art. cit.", p. 251.

which is to enable those who are under some real necessity to receive Communion after breaking the fast, such as people in mission territories, when the priest can visit them only at a late hour.[17]

In general, therefore, it can be stated that one who apart from any serious difficulty can attend an early Mass may not feel entitled to the use of this concession. But the impossibility or difficulty of attending an early Mass need not be physical or absolute. A practical impossibility, or also any real and serious inconvenience, would justify one in choosing a late hour for the reception of Holy Communion. In other words, any real inconvenience or serious difficulty which would deter the average well-disposed Catholic from fasting for a later Mass would suffice.

Article 3. The Laity Who Have to Travel a Long Distance to Church

The third cause which is presumed to give rise to the serious inconvenience that will enable the faithful to benefit from this concession is the long distance that has to be travelled to the church. This long distance has been interpreted by the Instruction for both priests and laymen as about two kilometers, which is equivalent to a mile and a quarter. A proportionately longer journey is necessary when a vehicle is used. In this regard, the difficulty of the journey and the physical condition must be taken into consideration.[18] As already shown in the case of priests, the distance of a mile and a quarter is the absolute minimum, so that persons who travel less may not benefit from this concession, regardless of the condition of their health, though undoubtedly they could benefit from the faculty given for those who are sick.[19]

There is some difficulty in deciding what would constitute a proportionately longer journey according to the type of vehicle used. However, it seems that it can be stated, as it was shown above, that any vehicular journey which consumes the same amount of time as a journey of a mile and a quarter on foot

17 Cf. Apostolic Constitution, n. 14; also n. 9.

18 Cf. Instruction, n. 10c.

19 Cf. Apostolic Constitution, n. 25, Norm II.

would be sufficient to entitle one to the use of this concession. In practice, this minimum amount of time appears to be approximately half an hour.

Must one choose the nearest church and the shortest way? While the text does not say so explicitly, nevertheless it gives some indication that the journey must be in some way necessary. This is evident from the phrase in the Constitution which refers to the "*longum iter quod suscipere debeant,*"[20] and from the phrase in the Instruction[21] which speaks of the "*longum iter peragendum.*" Both these phrases indicate that the journey is a necessary one for reaching the church, so that to undertake a long journey for the precise purpose of benefitting from the concession would not be justifiable. This opinion is corroborated by the majority of canonists.[22] However, it does not seem that the person must always go to the nearest church in order to benefit from this legislation. It seems that any reasonable cause would justify one in going to a more distant church, such as the journey made to a shrine, or a journey made for the purpose of a pilgrimage, or even the journey undertaken to attend Mass and to receive Communion with one's confrères in a sodality or a pious association. As long as the journey is really necessary and of such a nature as to cause the postulated serious inconvenience, one may justifiably feel entitled to the use of the concession.

[20] Cf. n. 28, Norm V.

[21] Cf. n. 10c.

[22] Ford, *The New Eucharistic Legislation,* p. 100; Werts, "The Eucharistic Fast," *Review for Religious,* XII (1953) 315; Hürth, *De Nova Disciplina Ieiuni Eucharistici,* p. 41; Conway, *The New Law of the Eucharistic Fast,* p. 56.

CHAPTER VI

EVENING MASSES

ARTICLE 1. WHO MAY PERMIT THEM AND UNDER WHAT CIRCUMSTANCES?

THE permission authorizing local ordinaries to allow evening Masses is one of the most far-reaching of the changes introduced by the new legislation, and is completely contrary to the law of the Code.[1] However, a somewhat similar privilege was granted to military chaplains for the benefit of military personnel on April 30, 1942,[2] so that the new legislation is not totally unprecedented.

Both the Constitution [3] and the Instruction [4] state that the faculty of allowing the celebration of evening Masses is granted to local ordinaries, and to them alone. Lest there should be any doubt as to whom this would include, the Instruction in the same paragraph refers the reader to canon 198, which enumerates those who are to be regarded as local ordinaries. The ordinaries included, apart from the Supreme Pontiff, for their respective territories are: residential bishops, not however titular or auxiliary ones unless they are also vicars general; abbots and prelates *nullius* as well as their vicars general, the apostolic administrator, vicars apostolic and prefects apostolic as well as those who in the place of the foregoing succeed to their right of government by either the prescription of law or approved constitutions. The law, therefore, excludes major religious superiors. The entire matter of granting permission for evening Masses is in the hands of the aforesaid ordinaries. It is part of their ordinary jurisdiction and consequently can be delegated in whole or in part.[5]

[1] Cf. canon 821, § 1.

[2] Cf. Bouscaren, *Canon Law Digest,* II, 670.

[3] Cf. n. 29, Norm VI.

[4] Cf. Prologue of n. 12.

[5] Cf. canon 199.

Even though this matter is entirely within the power of the local ordinary, he is not free to exercise it indiscriminately. The law places certain limits on the extent of his jurisdiction. The law demands as a *conditio sine qua non* for the use of this faculty that "the circumstances necessarily require it."[6] While the Constitution gives no indication of the meaning of this phrase, the Instruction interprets it to mean that the common good demands the celebration of Mass after midday. The Instruction furthermore enumerates examples of times and places where the common good so demands, as for "workmen in certain industries, who work their shifts even on feast days; for those categories of workers who are employed on feast day mornings, for example, those employed in seaport jobs; for those who have come from distant regions and gathered together in very large numbers for the celebration of some religious or social festivity." This list obviously is merely a demonstrative and not an exhaustive one, so that the local ordinary may permit an evening Mass whenever in his discretion the common good demands it and the circumstances necessarily require it. The ordinary and he alone has the duty and obligation of deciding when the common good so demands.

Authors are in agreement that a considerable number of factory workers on night shifts who would otherwise be deprived of assisting at Mass or could assist only with serious inconvenience would be a justifying reason for permitting Mass in the evening. The same would be true of nurses, police, customs officials, transportation workers, etc. In fact the ordinary could allow it for any group or category of people who work during the night or during the hours of morning Mass, and who because of the nature of their work are prevented from assisting at the Holy Sacrifice. The same would hold in missionary territory where, because of the great distances involved, the faithful would otherwise be prevented from assisting at Mass on Sundays and Holy Days of obligation.

While commentators are in agreement that, whenever a considerable number of the faithful would otherwise be deprived of Mass, the ordinary may permit it, they neglect to define what

[6] Cf. Apostolic Constitution, n. 26, Norm VI; also Instruction, n. 12.

that considerable number is. It seems that it could be stated as a general principle that the number of the faithful in the present case would be the same as the number that entitles the ordinary to permit a priest to binate on Sundays and Holy Days of obligation. Canonists usually state that about twenty persons would suffice to fulfill the requirement for bination. They believe that twenty persons would fulfill the condition decreed in canon 806, § 2, as a notable part of the faithful,[7] though in mission territories and in filial churches a smaller number would suffice.[8] This of course refers only to cases where the evening Mass is permitted by the ordinary to enable the faithful to fulfill their obligation of attending Mass on Sundays and Holy Days of obligation. The ordinary could not permit an evening Mass for twenty people who in the words of the Instruction[9] "come from distant regions in very large numbers for the celebration of a religious or social festivity," because by no stretch of the imagination could twenty people be regarded as a very large number even in mission territory. Moreover, this number when gathered for a religious or social festivity would in no way fulfill the aforesaid requirement, namely that "the circumstances necessarily require it." The examples of social and religious festivities usually cited by authors are: the inauguration of a President or a Governor; conventions of fraternal organizations such as the Knights of Columbus; a boy scout jamboree; a Holy Name or Marian rally; or the occasion of a national or diocesan Eucharistic congress, etc. In deciding this question the ordinary should never lose sight of the primary requirement, namely that the common good itself underlies the requirement for the evening Mass.

Could the ordinary permit an evening Mass for the benefit of

[7] Cf. Cappello, *Tractatus Canonico-Moralis de Sacramentis* (5 vols.; Vol. I, *De Sacramentis in Genere, de Baptismo, Confirmatione, et Eucharistiae*, 2. ed., Romae: Marietti, 1928), I, n. 732.

[8] Cf. Abbo-Hannan, *The Sacred Canons* (2 vols., St. Louis: Herder, 1952), I, 799-800, where reference is made to a case, mentioned by Gasparri, in which the Sacred Congregation of the Council declared that, where a filial church was involved, the need of only five persons in that filial Church sufficed for bination.

[9] Cf. Prologue to n. 12.

private individuals, as on the occasion of an ordination to the priesthood, for a priest's first Mass, or for a wedding ceremony? While such religious festivities might be the occasion for large numbers of people from distant regions assembling together, it is extremely difficult to visualize a case wherein " the circumstances necessarily require it." Such events can equally well take place in the forenoon. Furthermore, as already stated, the ordinary cannot permit evening Masses unless the common good requires it. The Masses here in question would be permitted not in the interest of the common good, but merely in the interest of private individuals. It seems that abuses in this matter have already arisen, and it was primarily to remedy these abuses and to forestall others of a similar nature that the Sacred Congregation of the Holy Office issued a special *Monitum* on March 22, 1955,[10] warning ordinaries against the granting of any permissions for evening Masses for the good of individuals or for the mere external adornment of some solemnity.

Another question that should be resolved is that of permitting evening Mass on the occasion of administering the sacrament of confirmation, and on the occasion of the closing of a Forty Hours' Devotion. This practice cannot be reconciled with the new legislation, inasmuch as it seems to be permitting evening Mass for the mere external adornment of a solemnity, the very practice the *Monitum* of March 22, 1955, forbade. Again it would be difficult to see how " the circumstances necessarily require it " or " the common good demands it." [11] Local ordinaries who wish to introduce or to continue this practice need the special permission of the Holy See, for they are not entitled by the new legislation to do so on their own authority.

Regarding the time of the evening Masses the Instruction explicitly states that they may not begin before four o'clock in the afternoon. The fact that the legislation does not mention any time beyond which they can be celebrated implies at least that

[10] Cf. *AAS*, XLVII (1955), 218.

[11] Connell (*The American Ecclesiastical Review*, CXXXVI [1957] 56) states that, since many persons could receive Communion at an evening Mass closing the Forty Hours' Devotion who could not be present at the morning Mass, such a Mass serves the common good.

they can be permitted any time up to midnight. The fact that the phrases "*horae vespertinae*" and "*missae vespertinae*" are mentioned does not necessarily exclude this. The distinction between evening and night is a relative thing depending on the latitude of the place and the customs of the people. Moreover, when the Mass of the Easter Vigil is celebrated before midnight and after eight o'clock it is considered a "*Missa Vespertina*" and is governed by the present legislation, and not by the Decree of January 11, 1952. There can no longer be any doubt about this because a Decree of the Holy Office on April 7, 1954, stated that, if the Mass of the Paschal Vigil is celebrated before midnight with the permission of the ordinary, the norms of the Apostolic Constitution *Christus Dominus* and of the Instruction of the Holy Office are to be observed.[12]

Again, there seems to be nothing in the law to prevent the local ordinary from permitting more than one evening Mass in one and the same Church on the same day. As long as the circumstances require it and the common good demands it, he may permit several Masses if they are necessary to satisfy the needs of the faithful.

Article. 2. The Fast Postulated for Evening Mass and Communion

In regard to the fast postulated for the clergy and the laity who celebrate or receive Communion at evening Masses, the law is not quite clear. There is an obvious discrepancy between the law as stated in the Apostolic Constitution and the Instruction. The Constitution[13] states that the clergy and the faithful must observe a fast of three hours from solid food and alcoholic beverages and a fast of one hour from other non-alcoholic beverages. The implication here is that the priests and the laity may take alcoholic beverages during meals and even outside of these meals provided they observe a three hour fast from alcoholic beverages. The Instruction,[14] on the other hand, clarifies the more

[12] Cf. *AAS,* XLVI (1954), 142. Cf. Bouscaren, *Canon Law Digest,* Supplement under canon 858.

[13] Cf. n. 29, Norm VI.

[14] Cf. n. 13.

general language of the Constitution to the effect that alcoholic drinks customary at meals, with the exception of liquors, are permitted in moderation "*inter refectionem,* permissam usque ad tres horas ante Missae vel communionis initium." Since the Instruction is the authentic interpretation of the Constitution, and since it was approved *in forma specifica,* thus becoming Pontifical law and having the same binding force as the Constitution itself, one would expect the law as found in the Instruction to be quite clear. However, such is not the case, and much has been written about the precise meaning of the phrase "inter refectionem, permissam usque ad tres horas ante Missae vel communionis initium."

The text in question is subject to three different interpretations. The first is that only one solid meal is allowed on the day when the priest or the faithful receive the Holy Eucharist at evening Mass, and it may be taken at any time during the day up to three hours beforehand. At this one meal non-spirituous alcoholic drink is permitted, and for the remainder of the day non-alcoholic liquid nourishment may be taken up to one hour beforehand. This interpretation does not seem intended by the legislator, for it would impose a rigorous ecclesiastical fast as well as a Eucharistic fast which in no way could be associated with Sundays, feast days and days of social or religious festivities. Yet the law was intended precisely for such days, occasions and events. Again, it would impose a severe hardship on both clergy and laity, which this law purports to lessen.

The second interpretation is that there is no restriction whatsoever on the desired number of solid meals accompanied with non-spirituous alcoholic beverages up to three hours beforehand. But apart from these meals only non-alcoholic liquid nourishment is allowed up to one hour beforehand.[15] While this view could be reconciled with the words of the Constitution itself, it can in no wise be reconciled with the wording of the Instruction, which speaks of *refectio,* and not *refectiones.* The obvious meaning of this is that non-spirituous alcoholic beverages can be taken only at one meal. The wording of the law which first appeared in the Vatican newspaper *L'Osservatore Romano* was re-

15 Cf. Mahoney, "Questions and Answers," *The Clergy Review,* XXXVIII (1953), 229ff.

vised in the official text which appeared in the *Acta Apostolicae Sedis,* and certainly if the legislator intended to allow non-spirituous alcoholic drinks at several meals he would have changed the word *refectio* to its plural form.

Furthermore, there is running all through the new legislation a note of warning against the use of alcohol before the reception of Holy Communion even when the alcohol is taken merely as a medication. Even though it is allowed at one meal, there is an express statement that it must be used in moderation, lest any abuse would creep in. The legislator, though lessening the rigor of the law, wants to preserve the traditional reverence for the Holy Eucharist, as can be seen from the warning issued to Ordinaries: "Ordinaries must carefully see to it that every abuse and irreverence toward the Most Blessed Sacrament be avoided." [16]

Again, the Instruction refers to "the beverages that may be taken before or after the aforesaid meal" and explicitly excludes the use of alcohol. The emphasis on the word "meal", referring to that one at which beer and wine may be taken, is a definite indication that the use of beer or wine is forbidden at all other meals. Likewise, it would seem incongruous to permit wine and beer at several meals and to forbid the priest who has to say an evening Mass to take the wine ablutions in the morning Mass.

The proper interpretation of this text, therefore, seems to be that the new legislation states it as a general principle that alcoholic drinks are completely forbidden before the reception of Holy Communion, regardless of the time of day when Communion is received. To that general law one exception is allowed. Where it is customary to have beer and wine at meals, that custom can be continued, but at one meal only. Like all exceptions to the general law, this one is subject to a strict interpretation.[17]

Now, since the law states that beer and wine may be taken at that meal which is permited up to three hours before Mass or Communion, as the case may be, it follows that the taking of wine and beer is allowed only once, and then only at the meal which is closest to the Mass or Communion. Thus, if a priest

[16] Cf. Instruction, n. 17.

[17] Cf. canon 19.

is saying Mass at nine o'clock in the evening and he has two full meals beforehand, for example one at noon and the other at five o'clock in the afternoon, he can have beer and wine at the five o'clock meal, but not at the noon meal.

Furthermore, this opinion is completely in keeping with the warning in the Instruction which states that " the interpretation of the Constitution and of this Instruction must faithfully keep to the text, and must not in any way enlarge the highly favorable faculties which have been granted." [18] Again, to interpret the twice used word *refectio* in the Instruction as equivalent to *refectiones* is by no means adhering to the text, but implies an extensive interpretation, which is absolutely forbidden. Moreover, to interpret the phrase " *inter refectionem,* permissam usque ad tres horas ante Missae vel communionis initium " as meaning that alcoholic beverages may be taken at any meal is to give it a liberal interpretation, whereas a strict one is demanded with reference to the stated exception to the general rule.

Another matter that deserves consideration here is the precise meaning of the word *liquores.* This word refers to distilled alcoholic beverages in contradistinction to fermented ones, such as beer and wine. The new legislation also excludes the use of synthetic liqueurs in which pure alcohol is added to the flavored syrups. In other words, regardless of the custom of the place or the need of the individual, all distilled liquors, whether in their natural form or diluted through the addition of some liquids, are absolutely forbidden from the previous midnight. However, solid foods prepared by the addition of brandy or other such distilled liquor may be taken, since the alcoholic beverages are alone forbidden.

Article 3. Days on Which the Ordinary May Permit Evening Masses

The Instruction furnishes a comprehensive list of the days on which the ordinary may permit evening Masses, provided the required conditions are fulfilled. He may grant permission for the celebrating of evening Masses:

1) On existing holy days of obligation in accordance with canon 1247, § 1;

[18] Cf. n. 19.

2) on suppressed holy days of obligation, according to the list published by the Sacred Congregation of the Council, December 28, 1919. The suppressed feasts are: Monday and Tuesday after Easter; Monday and Tuesday after Pentecost; Finding of the Holy Cross; Purification of the Blessed Virgin Mary; Annunciation; Nativity of the Blessed Virgin Mary; Dedication of St. Michael the Archangel; Nativity of St. John the Baptist; the feast days of the Holy Apostles Andrew, James, John, Thomas, Philip and James, Bartholomew, Matthew, Simon and Jude, Mathias; St. Stephen, Protomartyr; Holy Innocents; St. Lawrence, Martyr; St. Sylvester, Pope; St. Anne, Mother of the Blessed Virgin Mary; the Holy Patron of the Country; and the Holy Patron of the place; [19]

3) on the First Friday of each month;

4) on other solemnities which are celebrated with a great concourse of people;

5) on one day each week in addition to the above-mentioned days, if the good of special classes of persons demand it. There is one exception to the foregoing, not provided for in the Instruction, namely Holy Thursday. The question was asked whether Holy Thursday can be included among the days mentioned. The reply on March 21, 1953, stated: " The Sacred Congregation of Rites, after carefully considering the matter and hearing the opinion of the special Commission, decided to reply: '*Dilata*; and in the meantime let no change be introduced." [20]

Another question concerning the granting of permisson for evening Mass " on one day each week in addition to the above mentioned days, if the good of special classes of persons demands it " is whether the ordinary can permit it on one other day each week in all the churches in his diocese, or merely in one church on any particular day. As the law stands it seems that the bishop can permit it in several churches even in the same city on a particular day if the good of special classes of persons demands it. Or the bishop could permit it in different churches each day, provided he does not permit it in the same church on two days of any particular week. Thus " the one

[19] Cf. *AAS,* XII (1920), 42-43.

[20] Cf. Bouscaren, *Canon Law Digest,* Supplement, under canon 818.

day each week" refers to the church in which it is permitted, and not to the city or diocese in which the church is situated.[21]

In places where not the general law but the law of the missions is in force, ordinaries can permit evening Masses on all days of the week, under the same conditions.[22]

The law entitles the faithful, even if they are not of the number of those for whom the evening Mass may have been permitted, to freely approach the Holy Table during the aforesaid Mass, or just before and just after in accordance with canon 846, § 1, if they have observed the norms already stated concerning the Eucharistic fast.[23] From this it appears that it is not permissible to distribute Communion to a group of the faithful who are fasting according to the norms for evening Mass on an occasion when the bishop has given permission for evening Mass but there is no priest available to say it. The concession is granted only in connection with the actual celebration of the evening Mass. However, since Holy Communion may be distributed at a late hour for a reasonable cause,[24] the sick who have taken only liquids and medicine all day, and the faithful who have had only liquids all day up to one hour before the time of Communion would qualify under the law[25] and could be given Communion late in the day apart from any evening Mass.[26]

In conclusion it should be remembered that the Apostolic Constitution urges all those who avail themselves of the concessions to compensate for the reduced fast by means of prayer and penance. While this is not of strict obligation, it is something that should not be neglected, since it has always been the tradition of the Church that the mitigation of the law of fasting should be made up for by means of other good works.[27]

21 Cf. Hürth, *De Nova Disciplina Ieiunii Eucharistici*, p. 45.

22 Cf. Constitution, n. 30; Instruction, n. 16.

23 Cf. Instruction, n. 15.

24 Cf. canon 867, § 4.

25 Cf. Apostolic Constitution, n. 29, Norms II and V.

26 Cf. Ford, *The New Eucharistic Legislation*, p. 111.

27 Cf. Apostolic Constitution, n. 31.

CONCLUSIONS

1. The law of the Eucharistic Fast as found in the Code of Canon Law has been abrogated and is supplanted by the newly organized law of the Apostolic Constitution *Christus Dominus.*

2. The Apostolic Constitution and the accompanying Instruction are to be interpreted according to the norms of interpretation enacted in canon 18, which in practice means a liberal interpretation for texts of doubtful import in line with the benign intent of the lawgiver in enacting the new legislation.

3. The Instruction of the Holy Office of January 6, 1953, is an authentic interpretation of the Apostolic Constitution, having been approved by the Supreme Pontiff *in forma specifica.* The Apostolic Constitution and the accompanying Instruction are therefore one and the same law for the universal Church.

4. The phrase *grave incommodum* should be understood in the sense, not of a grave, but of any genuine, difficulty or as a serious inconvenience.

5. The law postulates a serious subjective inconvenience on the part of the priests and the laity before they qualify for the use of the granted concessions.

6. The confessor intended in the present legislation is a priest who in view of his possession of confessional jurisdiction could *hic et nunc* hear the confession of the person seeking advice, should that person decide to go to confession.

7. The required advice cannot be granted by letter, by telephone, or through a third party; nor can it be presumed unless there should arise a situation wherein the consultation would give rise to positive harm.

8. The required favorable judgment or decision cannot by means of a single act be rendered by a confessor for an entire group of persons though their status and condition be attended with the same set of circumstances.

9. There is no limit to the amount of liquid nutrition for which allowance is made in the new law.

10. Solid food or alcoholic beverages, even when prescribed by a physician, are never to be regarded as true medicine.

11. Patent medicines with an alcoholic base may rightly be regarded as medicines.

12. Serious sickness is not envisioned in the present legislation when it makes provision for the sick and infirm, so that persons who suffer from temporary infirmities, such as those arising from a severe headache, can be regarded as sick.

13. Consultation of a confessor is not required on the part of sick priests who wish to take liquid food or medicine before the celebration of Mass or the reception of Holy Communion.

14. A person who has taken liquid food or medicine may subsequently still consult the confessor. However, the consultation must precede the reception of Holy Communion.

15. A person who is the guilty cause of his own sickness cannot avail himself of the concessions.

16. The required serious subjective inconvenience must arise in every case from one of the comprehensively listed causes specified in the law, and not from the Eucharistic fast as such.

17. For priests about to celebrate Mass, nine o'clock is set as an absolute late hour, and the time is to be reckoned physically and not morally. In the case of the laity, the lateness of the hour may be considered according to a relative norm.

18. Priests and laity may use a relative norm in gauging the period of time that is essential to the notion of " a long period of time." Two hours, when measured simply by the yardstick of duration (*ratione temporis*) or one hour when appraised in the light of intense activity (*ratione intensitatis*) could be accepted as reasonable in most cases.

19. The distance of a mile and a quarter stated in the law is to be regarded as the minimum. The proportionately longer journey when a vehicle is used would be a journey which consumes at least the same amount of time as a journey of a mile and a quarter on foot.

20. The phrase " a priest who has to say another Mass " must be interpreted to mean that there is some obligation to say the second Mass. Thus a priest who took the ablutions inadvertently in the earlier Mass is not allowed to say a second Mass for furthering or satisfying his own devotion (*ex devotione*).

21. The obligation of deciding when the common good demands an evening Mass rests with the local ordinary.

22. The local ordinary could permit an evening Mass for the benefit of twenty persons on Sundays and Holy Days of obligation. In a mission church a smaller number would suffice.

23. The clergy who celebrate evening Masses and the laity who receive Communion at the evening Masses are allowed the use of such alcoholic beverages as beer and wine during the meal that is permitted up until at least three hours beforehand, but at that meal alone.

(*The above conclusions refer exclusively to the Apostolic Constitution Christus Dominus and have no bearing on the subsequent law as set down in the Appendix.*)

APPENDIX

THE MOTU PROPRIO *SACRAM COMMUNIONEM*

Introduction

On March 19, 1957, His Holiness Pope Pius XII promulgated the Motu Proprio *Sacram Communionem,* abrogating the generous and far-reaching concessions granted in the Apostolic Constitution *Christus Dominus* of January 6, 1953, and supplanting them with a completely new set of laws binding Catholics throughout the universal Church. This new Eucharistic law took effect on March 25, 1957.

The new law embodied in this Motu Proprio deals primarily with two things. First, it extends the liberal concessions granted by the Apostolic Constitution *Christus Dominus* of January 6, 1953, regarding the Eucharistic fast. Secondly, it empowers local ordinaries to permit priests to celebrate afternoon Masses on every day of the year " whenever the spiritual good of a notable part of the faithful demands it."

In the introductory paragraphs of the Motu Proprio the Supreme Pontiff stated the reasons which prompted him to enact the present legislation. They are twofold. In the first place the hierarchy had testified to the fact that the concessions of 1953 had borne abundant spiritual fruits. At the same time the bishops requested a further relaxation, so that the fruits already discernible might continue to grow. The second reason mentioned in the Motu Proprio is the same as that already stated in the Apostolic Constitution *Christus Dominus,* namely, the ever-changing conditions of modern industrial and social life. Undoubtedly the Holy Father had another reason, which he did not mention. During the last century an ever-growing tide of materialism has threatened to engulf the Church. This tide can be stemmed only by greater devotion to Christ in the Eucharist, which can be shown in no better way than by the frequent and daily reception of the Eucharist on the part of the faithful. Until the promulgation of the present law, however, the daily reception of Holy Communion was extremely difficult for many persons. The present law has obviated all such difficulties, so that the daily reception of Communion is relatively easy for the vast majority of Catholics.

In promulgating the new law the Sovereign Pontiff also called the attention of the clergy and the faithful to some pertinent facts regarding the use of the new concessions. He exhorted all, both the priests and the faithful, if they are able to do so, to continue " to observe the venerable and time-honored form of the Eucharistic fast before the celebration of Mass and the reception of Holy Communion." Furthermore, he urged all who use the new concessions to become " shining examples of a Christian life through their works of penance and charity." While both these statements are counsels of perfection without any juridical binding force, nevertheless they are not to be ignored. It has always been the tradition of the Church that the mitigation of the law of fasting should be compensated for by means of other good works. Consequently, the clergy and the faithful should endeavour to put these exhortations into practice, since they represent the mind of the Church, which is constantly striving for the sanctification of its members.

The new legislation contains four decrees, each of which will be considered separately in the following articles.

MOTU PROPRIO *

Indulta a Constitutione Apostolica "Christus Dominus" Extenduntur

SACRAM Communionem ut Christifideles frequenter recipere possent et quo facilius praecepto de audiendo Sacro diebus festis satisfacerent, ineunte anno MCMLIII, Constitutionem Apostolicam *Christus Dominus* promulgavimus, qua ieiunii Eucharistici disciplinam mitigavimus; Ordinariis autem locorum tribuimus facultatem permittendi Missae celebrationem et sacrae Communionis receptionem horis postmeridianis, certis sub conditionibus.

Tempus vero servandi ieiunii ante Missam vel sacram Communionem, quae horis postmeridianis celebretur vel recipiatur, coarctavimus ad tres horas quoad cibum solidum et ad unam horam quoad potum non alcoholicum.

Uberibus fructibus ex hac concessione captis permoti, Episcopi maximas Nobis egerunt gratias et plures eorum, ad maius fidelium bonum, instantibus et iteratis precibus postularunt facultatem permittendi quotidie Missae celebrationem horis postmeridianis. Postularunt insuper ut idem statueremus tempus ieiunii servandi ante Missam vel sacram Communionem, quae horis antemeridianis celebraretur vel reciperetur.

Nos, attendentes ad notabiles mutationes, quas ordinatio laborum ac munerum publicorum necnon universae vitae societatis passa est, instantibus Sacrorum Antistitum precibus satisfacere censuimus atque ideo decrevimus:

1. Ordinarii locorum, exceptis Vicariis Generalibus sine mandato speciali, permittere possunt Missae celebrationem horis postmeridianis quotidie, si bonum spirituale notabilis partis christifidelium id postulet.

* *AAS*, XXXXIX (1957), 177 and 178.

MOTU PROPRIO

The Indults Granted by the Apostolic Constitution Christus Dominus are Extended

Early in the year 1953 We promulgated the Apostolic Constitution *Christus Dominus,* by virtue of which We lessened the rigor of the Eucharistic fast, so that the faithful could receive Holy Communion more frequently and fulfill the precept of hearing Holy Mass on Holy Days of obligation more easily. For this reason We granted to local ordinaries the faculty of permitting the celebration of Mass and the reception of Holy Communion in the afternoon, provided certain conditions were fulfilled.

We limited the period of time for the observance of the Eucharistic fast before the celebration of Mass and the reception of Holy Communion in the afternoon to three hours from solid food and to one hour from non-alcoholic liquids.

The bishops, mindful of the abundant fruits gleaned through these concessions, expressed to Us their profound gratitude, and many of them have persistently and repeatedly asked Us to grant them the faculty of allowing afternoon Masses daily, in view of the great benefit which the faithful would derive from it. They have requested Us, moreover, to decree the same period of obligatory fasting prior to the celebration of Mass and the reception of Holy Communion in the morning hours that We had specified for afternoon Masses.

Mindful of the notable changes which have occurred in private and public working conditions as well as in all branches of social life, We deemed it advisable to comply with the insistent requests of the bishops and have therefore decreed:

1. Local ordinaries, with the exception of vicars general apart from the possession of a special mandate, may permit the celebration of Holy Mass every day after midday whenever the spiritual good of a considerable number of the faithful demands it.

2. Tempus ieiunii Eucharistici servandi a sacerdotibus ante Missam et a christifidelibus ante sacram Communionem, horis sive antemeridianis sive postmeridianis, limitatur ad tres horas quoad cibum solidum et potum alcoholicum, ad unam autem horam quoad potum non alcoholicum: aquae sumptione ieiunium non frangitur.

3. Ieiunium Eucharisticum per tempus supradictum servare tenentur etiam qui Missam celebrant vel sacram Communionem recipiunt media nocte aut primis diei horis.

4. Infirmi, quamvis non decumbant, potum non alcoholicum et veras ac proprias medicinas, sive liquidas sive solidas, ante Missae celebrationem vel Eucharistiae receptionem sine temporis limite sumere possunt.

At enixe hortamur sacerdotes et christifideles, qui id praestare valeant ut venerandam ac vetustam Eucharistici ieiunii formam ante Missam vel sacram Communionem servent.

Omnes denique, qui his facultatibus perfruentur, collatum beneficium pro viribus rependere satagant fulgentioribus christianae vitae exemplis, praesertim poenitentiae et caritatis operibus.

Praescripta, quae in his Litteris Apostolicis Motu Proprio datis continentur, vim suam exerunt a die vigesimo quinto mensis martii, in festo Annuntiationis Beatae Mariae Virginis.

Contrariis quibuslibet non obstantibus etiam speciali mentione dignis.

Datum Romae apud Sanctum Petrum, die XIX mensis Martii, in festo S. Ioseph, Ecclesiae Universalis Patroni, anno MDCCCCLVII, Pontificatus Nostri undevigesimo.

PIUS PP. XII

2. The period of time for the observance of the Eucharistic fast by priests who wish to celebrate Mass and by the faithful who wish to receive Holy Communion, whether in the forenoon or in the afternoon, is limited to three hours for solid food and alcoholic beverages, and to one hour for non-alcoholic beverages. The Eucharistic fast is not broken through the consumption of water.

3. The Eucharistic fast for the length of time above specified must be observed even by those who celebrate Mass or receive Holy Communion at midnight or in the early hours of the day.

4. The sick, even though they be not confined to bed, and apart from all temporal restrictions or limitations, may take non-alcoholic beverages and also medicines, if these be truly and really such, in either liquid or solid form, before the celebration of Mass and the reception of Holy Communion.

We earnestly exhort the priests and the faithful, if they be able to do so, to observe the venerable and time-honored form of the Eucharistic fast before the celebration of Mass and the reception of Holy Communion.

Let all, then, who make use of these faculties compensate for the conferred benefit as best they can by becoming shining examples of a Christian life, especially through their works of penance and charity.

The prescriptions as given in this Motu Proprio begin to bind on March 25, 1957, the Feast of the Annunciation of the Blessed Virgin Mary.

Every disposition whatsoever to the contrary, though it appear deserving of special mention, is hereby abrogated.

Given at Rome at St. Peter's, on March 19, the Feast of St. Joseph, the Patron of the Universal Church, in the year 1957, the nineteenth of Our Pontificate.

PIUS PP. XII

CANONICAL COMMENTARY

ARTICLE 1. WHO MAY PERMIT AFTERNOON MASSES AND UNDER WHAT CIRCUMSTANCES?

Ordinarii locorum, exceptis Vicariis Generalibus sine mandato speciali, permittere possunt Missae celebrationem horis postmeridianis quotidie, si bonum spirituale notabilis partis christifidelium id postulet.

Under the law decreed in the Apostolic Constitution *Christus Dominus,* the faculty of permitting the celebration of evening Masses was granted to local ordinaries and to them alone. Thus vicars general enjoyed the power of granting the necessary permission whenever the requisite conditions were fulfilled. This faculty has now been restricted, and vicars general apart from the possession of a special mandate are expressly excluded.

The ordinaries, therefore, who can permit afternoon Masses under the Motu Proprio *Sacram Communionem* apart from the Supreme Pontiff are: residential bishops, not however auxiliary or titular ones, even though they are also vicars general; abbots and prelates *nullius,* the apostolic administrator, vicars apostolic and prefects apostolic as well as those who in the place of the foregoing succeed to their right of government by either the prescription of law or approved constitutions. Major religious superiors are excluded for the reason that they are not local ordinaries.[1]

The matter of granting permission for the celebration of afternoon Masses is in the hands of the aforesaid ordinaries. It is part of their ordinary jurisdiction, and consequently can be delegated in whole or in part.[2]

The Apostolic Constitution *Christus Dominus* enabled local ordinaries to permit evening Masses, provided such Masses did not begin before four o'clock in the afternoon. The Motu Pro-

[1] Cf. canon 198.

[2] Cf. canon 199, § 1.

prio of Pius XII has extended this period of time, so that now local ordinaries may permit priests to begin these Masses any time in the afternoon. Furthermore, since the legislator does not mention any time beyond which they may not be celebrated, it seems that they may be permitted for any time up to midnight. This follows from the fact that the Sacred Congregation of the Holy Office on April 7, 1954, decreed that if the Mass of the Paschal Vigil is celebrated before midnight with the permission of the ordinary, the norms of the Apostolic Constitution *Christus Dominus* and of the Instruction of the Holy Office were to be observed.[3] In other words, according to this reply all Masses beginning after four o'clock in the afternoon were to be regarded as evening Masses, no matter when they began.

Since the present law is an extension of the Apostolic Constitution *Christus Dominus,* as is evident from the title of the Motu Proprio, it follows that afternoon Masses may be allowed any time from noon to midnight whenever the requisite conditions are present.

It should be noted, however, that the law of the Code of Canon Law which forbids the celebration of Mass earlier than an hour before dawn or later than an hour after noon still obliges.[4] This is obvious from the fact that Mass may not be celebrated even under the present indult in the afternoon hours without the special permission of the local ordinary, and this permission may be granted only when the spiritual good of a notable part of the faithful demands it. Thus, bishops still may not allow Mass to begin earlier than an hour before dawn without the special permission of the Holy See.

Even though the Motu Proprio *Sacram Communionem* entitles local ordinaries to permit the celebration of afternoon Masses at any hour from noon until midnight, it does so only when "the spiritual good of a considerable part of the faithful demands it." This is another instance wherein the present law differs from the former one. The Apostolic Constitution on January 6, 1953, em-

[3] Cf. *AAS,* XLVI (1954), 142; Cf. Bouscaren, *Canon Law Digest, Supplement,* under canon 858.

[4] Canon 821, § 1.

powered ordinaries to allow evening Masses "when the circumstances necessarily require it," and the concomitant Instruction interpreted this phrase to mean that the good of special classes of people demanded the celebration of Mass in the afternoon.[5]

The phrase "*notabilis pars fidelium*" is not a new one. The same expression is used in the Code, where it is stated that the bishop may permit a priest to binate on Sundays and Holy Days of obligation whenever a notable part of the faithful would otherwise be deprived of the opportunity of fulfilling the precept of assisting at Mass.[6]

It is the common opinion of canonists that about twenty persons would suffice to fulfill this requirement for bination. In other words, twenty persons would be considered a notable part of the faithful, though in mission territories and in filial churches a smaller number would suffice.[7]

It seems the legislator in the present legislation advisedly chose the phrase "*notabilis pars fidelium*," and consequently it must be interpreted in the light of its former juridical use and interpretation. Thus, it can be categorically stated that the local ordinary may allow afternoon Masses at any hour from noon until midnight whenever in his judgment he believes that the spiritual good of approximately twenty persons will demand it. The writer is here referring to areas where the Church is well established. In mission territories and in filial churches afternoon Mass may be permitted for the benefit of even five persons. Moreover, the ordinary may permit afternoon Masses on every day of the year, which again is an extension of the former law, which restricted it to certain specified days. In fact, under the present concession the ordinary may permit several afternoon

[5] Cf. Apostolic Constitution, n. 26, Norm VI; also Instruction, n. 12.

[6] Cf. canon 806, § 2.

[7] Cf. Cappello, *Tractatus Canonico-Moralis de Sacramentis* (5 vols.; Vol. I, *De Sacramentis in Genere, de Baptismo, Confirmatione, et Eucharistiae,* 2. ed., Romae: Marietti, 1928), I, n. 732; also Abbo-Hannan, *The Sacred Canons* (2 vols., St. Louis: Herder, 1952), I, 799-800, where reference is made to a case mentioned by Gasparri, in which the Sacred Congregation of the Council declared that, where a filial church was involved, the need of only five persons in that filial church sufficed for bination.

Masses in the same church on any or every day of the year provided " the spiritual good of a considerable number of the faithful demands it."

The question whether a local ordinary may permit evening Masses on the occasion of a wedding, of an ordination to the priesthood, or of the first Mass of a newly ordained priest, may be debated. Under the former concessions it seems that the *Monitum* of March 22, 1955, forbade this practice, inasmuch as it warned ordinaries against the granting of evening Masses for the good of individuals or for the mere external adornment of some solemnity.[8] The only requisite under the present law, however, is that " the spiritual good of a notable part of the faithful demands it." Whenever this condition is verified, it seems that such permissions may be given. Thus, if the ordinary foresees that even as few as twenty persons in a parish church would benefit by this concession, or even a smaller number in mission and filial churches, he may grant the required permission. Moreover, since the present law abrogates those parts of the former law which are contrary to it, as is evident from the abrogating clause " *contrariis quibuslibet non obstantibus, etiam speciale mentione dignis,*" it seems that it also abrogates the *Monitum* of March 22, 1955, so that afternoon Masses may now be allowed, not only for the benefit of the common good, but also for the benefit of private individuals. The only condition is that the spiritual good of a notable part of the faithful demands it.

Closely allied to the foregoing problem is that of allowing evening Mass in convents, orphanages, hospitals and similar charitable institutions. Frequently it is extremely difficult for the sisters and nurses in such institutions to assist at morning Mass and at the same time to take adequate care of their charges. Where the circumstances are such, there seems to be nothing in the present law to prevent local ordinaries from permitting afternoon Masses for the benefit of such categories of persons. As long as the condition expressed in the law is fulfilled, the local ordinary may give the required permission.

What then is to be thought of the granting of permission for afternoon Masses for the benefit of College and University stu-

[8] Cf. *AAS,* XLVII (1955), 218.

dents? It frequently happens, especially in the United States of America, that College and University students are required to be present at their classes as early as eight o'clock in the morning. Many of these students travel long distances to school, and it would be seriously difficult for them to assist at Mass and then to return home for breakfast before they set out for school. Furthermore, they frequently have to attend classes until noon. Many of these students are desirous and willing to assist at daily Mass, but because of circumstances beyond their control they are unable to do so. Such students moreover need the many graces which can be derived from assistance at the Holy Sacrifice, especially those who are exposed to the secularism and materialism of public and State Universities. It does not seem to be stretching the law to say that local ordinaries could permit the celebration of afternoon Masses in the oratories of secular and Catholic universities for the benefit of such students, as long as the condition expressed in the law is verified.

Thus it seems that the only consideration required is the spiritual good of a notable part of the faithful, and whenever this condition is fulfilled the local ordinary need have no scruple in granting the required permission.

Article 2. The Eucharistic Fast for the Priests and the Laity

Tempus ieiunii eucharistici servandi a sacerdotibus ante Missam et a christifidelibus ante sacram Communionem, horis sive antemeridianis sive postmeridianis, limitatur ad tres horas quoad cibum solidum et potum alcoholicum, ad unam autem horam quoad potum non alcoholicum; aquae sumptione ieiunium non frangitur.

The Motu Proprio *Sacram Communionem,* just as its forerunner the Apostolic Constitution *Christus Dominus,* decrees as a general principle for all that the Eucharistic fast is not broken by the consumption of water. Furthermore it sets no time limit, so that water may be taken up to the very moment that Holy Communion is being received.

There is, however, one accidental difference between the present law and the former one. While the former law stated as a general principle that the consumption of natural water did not break the fast, and the accompanying Instruction defined natural water as water without the addition of any element whatsoever, the present law makes no such distinction.[9]

There was some doubt under the former law about the exact meaning of natural water, and canonists were not in agreement as to the lawfulness of using tap water and water to which the public health authorities had added purifying substances for the protection of the health of the citizens. This and similar disputed matters are no longer a source of difficulty. As long as the substance can be judged in the common estimation of men as fulfilling the notion of water, it may be consumed without a violation of the Eucharistic fast. Thus every type and kind of water, even mineral water, carbonated water and chemically purified water may now be used.

The new legislation lays it down as a general principle that priests may now take solid foods and alcoholic beverages up to three hours, and liquids up to one hour, before the beginning of the celebration of Mass. The same rule binds the laity, except that the three-hour and one-hour periods are to be measured from the time they receive Holy Communion. This is a notable extension of the former law. Whereas the former law allowed the three-hour and one-hour limitation only when Mass was celebrated and Holy Communion received in the afternoon, the present law extends it regardless of the time of day or night that Mass is celebrated or Holy Communion is received.

Again, it should be noted that the three-hour and one-hour periods are to be computed mathematically, so that all moral approximation is forbidden. Just as a person who under the law of the Code deliberately received Communion after taking food or drink even one moment after midnight sinned gravely, so under the present law a priest who would knowingly begin Mass or a lay person who would deliberately receive Communion before the stipulated period of fasting time has elapsed would also be guilty of serious sin.

Under the former law priests who celebrated evening Masses and the laity who received Holy Communion in the afternoon or

[9] Cf. Apostolic Constitution, n. 24, Norm I; also Introduction of the Instruction.

evening hours were forbidden the use of alcoholic beverages from the previous midnight, with the exception of wine and beer at the principal meal. This law has now been abrogated, so that the priests and the laity may take alcoholic beverages of any kind whatsoever up to three hours before the celebration of Mass and the reception of Holy Communion respectively. The present legislation makes no distinction between light beverages and liquors, whereas the former law expressly excluded liquors of every kind.[10]

In this matter the prohibition in the earlier law itself served as a protection for the Holy Eucharist against any irreverence or abuse, whereas the present law leaves it to the individual conscience to guard against all abuse. Consequently, the clergy and the laity will need to exert the greatest caution. It would be a source of great scandal if a priest were to offer Mass or a lay person were to receive Holy Communion while under the influence of alcohol, even though only slightly so. The moral virtue of temperance must be observed, so that those who wish to receive Holy Communion must not eat or drink to excess. Indeed, the Holy Father exhorted the faithful, if they could do so, to observe the venerable and time-honored form of the Eucharistic fast.

Regarding the use of non-alcoholic liquids the time specified for priests who wish to celebrate Mass is one hour before the beginning of Mass and for the laity one hour before the reception of Holy Communion. There still may be doubts in the minds of some as to the precise meaning of liquids. It seems, however, that the term may be interpreted in the light of the reply of the Sacred Congregation of the Holy Office on September 7, 1897, which stated that liquids could include broth, coffee, or also liquids in which there were mixed some substances such as semolina, crumbled bread, etc., as long as the mixture did not lose its liquid character.[11] In the present context, therefore, liquids can be interpreted to mean any substance which according to common parlance is said to be drunk rather than eaten. Thus,

[10] Cf. Instruction, n. 13.

[11] *Fontes*, n. 1192.

heavier liquids, such as egg nog and milk shakes, may be used even though some undissolved solids remain in them, provided that the complete substance can be regarded as a potable liquid.

Finally, the law no longer demands the advice of a confessor, nor the presence of a serious inconvenience for the use of these concessions. It is now the general law of the Church that solid foods and alcoholic beverages may be taken by priests up to three hours before the beginning of Mass, and liquids, up to one hour. For the laity the same law applies except that the three-hour and one-hour periods are measured from the time Holy Communion is to be received. The only exception to the foregoing rule is the reception of Viaticum, which requires no fast at all, and the reception of Holy Communion to prevent irreverance to the Blessed Sacrament.[12]

Article 3. The Fast for Midnight Masses and Communion

> *Ieiunium Eucharisticum per tempus supradictum servare tenentur etiam qui Missam celebrant vel sacram Communionem recipiunt media nocte aut primis diei horis.*

From the very first centuries, if not from Apostolic times, midnight had been set as the point from which the observance of the Eucharistic fast for the celebration of Mass and the reception of Holy Communion was to be computed. Consequently, when Mass was begun at midnight or in the very early hours of the morning, or when Communion was received at midnight or in the early succeeding hours, the fast bound from midnight only. Therefore, for those receiving Communion at the stroke of midnight there was no period of fasting whatsoever. This law has now been abrogated, and the present law decrees that no matter at what hour of the day or the night Mass is celebrated or Holy Communion received, the period of fasting is three hours from solid food and alcoholic beverages and one hour from non-alcoholic beverages. In making one law that applies to all Masses and Communions, the Supreme Pontiff has assured a world-wide and uniform practice that can be easily applied and easily understood by all.

[12] Cf. canon 858, § 1.

Article 4. The Eucharistic Fast for the Sick

Infirmi, quamvis non decumbant, potum non alcoholicum et veras ac proprias medicinas, sive liquidas sive solidas, ante Missae celebrationem vel Eucharistiae receptionem sine temporis limite sumere possunt.

In this rule the Supreme Pontiff demonstrated again his paternal solicitude for the sick and infirm by granting a further concession to them. The sick, whether priests or laity, are permitted to take anything to drink that is non-alcoholic up to the beginning of Mass or the reception of Holy Communion respectively. They are also permitted to take medicine, whether in solid or in liquid form, up to the beginning of Mass or the reception of Holy Communion.

The Apostolic Constitution *Christus Dominus* granted a similar concession, but the advice of a confessor was required in every case. Such advice is no longer required, and the sick may avail themselves of this privilege whenever they can be classified as such.

The type of sickness envisioned by the legislator may be a source of difficulty. Does the law refer to a serious sickness only, or also to a sickness light in nature and character? In the first place it should be noted that the law itself states that the question of being confined to bed has nothing whatsoever to do with the interpretation of the word *infirmus.* This Latin word is best translated with the English infirm, since it has a wider connotation than either the words sick or ill. Furthermore, it seems that the legislator advisedly chose the word *infirmus* rather than *aegrotus,* which latter term has a much narrower connotation. Thus it may be stated that the infirmity here adverted to is not of as serious a nature as that which receives mention in the Code of Canon Law.[13]

Moreover, inasmuch as the phrase " *quamvis non decumbant* " is used, the implication is that the legislator is using the word as a more extensive term. Again, the law entitles priests who are going to say Mass to use the faculty, which is an indication that a grave sickness is not envisioned, inasmuch as priests who are

[13] Cf. canon 858, § 2.

seriously ill are not likely to celebrate Mass. Therefore it seems that even a temporary infirmity, such as that which results from a severe headache, suffices.

The sick may not only take non-alcoholic liquids up to the beginning of Mass and the reception of Holy Communion, but they may also take medicines, if these be truly and really such, in either liquid or solid form. In this matter, just as in the case of liquids, the criterion for deciding whether a given substance is medicine or not is the common estimation of men. Should the findings of science be in conflict with the common estimation of men, the preference rests with the latter.[14] Thus, if a doctor were to prescribe solid foods as a medicine for diabetic patients, they would not be justified in taking them during the three hours preceding Communion, because by no stretch of the imagination could solid foods be regarded as medicine in the common estimation of men.

Furthermore, it would be difficult to visualise sick persons unable to fast from solid foods for three hours, especially since they are allowed heavier liquids up to the very moment that Communion is to be received. Should such cases arise, they should seek an apostolic indult, for the present law does not seem to include such cases. Thus, whatever substance can be regarded as medicine in the common estimation of men, whether of a liquid or of a solid nature, may be taken up to the beginning of Mass or the reception of Holy Communion.

There is room, perhaps, for speculation whether alcoholic drinks may be taken during the three hours preceding the celebration of Mass and the reception of Holy Communion when they are prescribed by a physician for medicinal purposes. This question was a source of much debate under the former law, and undoubtedly the question will be discussed further in the interpretation of the present one.

The text of the law, however, seems quite clear. It states that the sick may take medicines, if these be truly and really such, in either liquid or solid form, without any time limitation before the celebration of Mass and the reception of Holy Communion.

[14] Cf. Anglin, *The Eucharistic Fast*, p. 63.

It is extremely difficult to see how such beverages as whiskey and brandy could ever be classified as true and real medicine in the common estimation of men. It is possible that such liquids may have some medicinal value, but the average individual would not classify them as medicine, even were a doctor to prescribe them for a patient. They would be classified as alcoholic beverages regardless of their curative value, even though scientifically they might be regarded as medicine. Furthermore, it is extremely doubtful whether medical science in modern times ever prescribes alcoholic beverages as real and true medicine.

The evident purpose of the exclusion of alcoholic beverages is the prevention of abuses. It seems useless to assert that just because a doctor prescribes them the danger would thereby be averted. This is a definite instance wherein the principle enunciated in canon 21 is applicable, namely, that laws when made for safeguarding against a common danger must be observed even though there be no danger in a particular case.

Again, the reverence demanded for the reception of the Holy Eucharist would of itself suggest some such limitation, inasmuch as alcoholic beverages lessen the powers of concentration in a healthy individual and would undoubtedly do so to a greater degree in the case of the sick. Therefore it must be concluded that alcoholic beverages, even when prescribed by a physician, can never be taken during the three-hour prescribed period of fast.

On the other hand, it seems that medicines containing some alcohol may be used, provided they can be regarded as really and truly such. Thus patent medicines, even though they have some alcoholic content, may be taken on one's own initiative or on the advice of a doctor, provided they would be regarded as real medicine in the common estimation of men.

A more difficult problem, however, and one not mentioned in the Motu Proprio Sacram Communionem, is the question of taking the ablutions in the first Mass when a priest binates. Under the law as decreed in the Apostolic Constitution *Christus Dominus,* priests who binated or trinated were entitled to take the water ablutions in the earlier Masses.[15] The concomitant Instruction of the Holy Office in interpreting this concession

[15] Cf. n. 27, Norm, IV.

limited it in two cases.[16] It stated that one who celebrated three Masses on Christmas Day or on All Souls' Day was obliged to observe the rubrics with regard to the ablutions. This law implied that when some period of time elapsed between the Masses, the ablutions with water could be taken.

The same law also stated that a priest when under obligation to binate or trinate was not forbidden to say the second or third Mass, if at the earlier Mass he inadvertently took wine also in the ablutions. This was interpreted to mean that the priest had some specific obligation to say the second or the third Mass. Thus, a priest who took the wine ablutions inadvertently in the earlier Mass was not allowed to say a second Mass for furthering or satisfying his own devotion.

The Motu Proprio *Sacram Communionem* omits all reference to the taking of the ablutions in cases of bination and trination. The question to be resolved therefore is: does the law of the Apostolic Constitution *Christus Dominus* on this particular point continue to bind or has it lost its earlier binding force? At first sight it could seem that the law of 1953 has been totally repealed, inasmuch as in the present Motu Proprio the abrogating clause, "*contrariis quibuslibet non obstantibus, etiam speciali mentione dignis,*" is used. Thus it could seem that a priest who wished to binate or trinate might allowably take the ablutions with water in the earlier Masses even on Christmas Day and on All Souls' Day, despite the earlier applicable prohibitory ruling, when these Masses were said in an unbroken and immediate succession. In addition, if one were to follow this view, whenever a period of three full hours elapses between the Masses the priest could take wine ablutions in the earlier Masses, inasmuch as the present prescription calls simply for a three-hour period of fast from alcoholic beverages.

It appears, however, that this is neither the meaning of the text of the law nor the mind of the legislator. The abrogating clause, which states that "*every disposition whatsoever to the contrary, though it appear worthy of special mention,* is hereby abrogated," implies at least that the dispositions of the law which are not contrary to the present law still continue to bind.

[16] Cf. nn. 7 and 8.

Since no mention is made of the ablutions, and since in consequence thereof the law of the Apostolic Constitution is not contrary to the present law, it is rightfully to be concluded that priests when binating or trinating are still bound by the former dispositions.

Furthermore, since the Motu Proprio *Sacram Communionem* is an extension of the indults granted in 1953 (as is evident from the title "*Indulta a Constitutione Apostolica 'Christus Dominus' extenduntur*"), but abstracts from all reference to the law concerning the ablutions, it follows that that portion of the law was not subjected to any change and accordingly must still be considered as binding.

BIBLIOGRAPHY

Sources

Acta Apostolicae Sedis, Commentarium Officiale, Romae, 1909-

Acta Sanctae Sedis, 41 vols., Romae, 1865-1908.

Bouscaren, T. Lincoln, *The Canon Law Digest,* 3 vols. and Supplements through 1955, Milwaukee: Bruce & Co., 1934-1949-1953-1954-1955-1956.

Canones et Decreta Concilii Tridentini, Taurini, 1913.

Codex Iuris Canonici, Pii X Pontificis Maximi iussu digestus, Benedicti Papae XV auctoritate promulgatus, Praefatione, Fontium Annotatione et Indice Analytico-Alphabetico, ab Emo Petri Card. Gasparri Auctus, Romae: Typis Polyglottis Vaticanis, 1917; Reimpressio, 1934.

Codicis Iuris Canonici Fontes, cura Emi Petri Card. Gasparri editi, 9 vols., Romae (postea Civitate Vaticana): Typis Polyglottis Vaticanis, 1923-1939 (Vols. VII-IX, ed. cura et studio Emi Iustiniani Card. Serédi).

Codificazione Canonica Orientale, Fonti, Serie I, 13 fasc., Serie II, 18 fasc., *Fontes,* Series III, Vols. I, II, III, V, Pars II, VI, VII, Pars II, Citta del Vaticano: Tipografia Poliglotta Vaticana, 1930-

Decretum Gratiani emendatum et notationibus illustratum cum glossis, Gregorii XIII, Pont. Max., iussu editum, 2 vols., Romae, 1582.

Mansi, Joannes, *Sacrorum Conciliorum Nova et Amplissima Collectio,* 53 vols. in 60, Parisiis, Arnhemii, Lipsiae, 1901-1927.

Reference Works

Abbo, John, A.-Hannan, Jerome, D., *The Sacred Canons,* 2 vols., St. Louis: Herder, 1952.

Anglin, Thomas Francis, *The Eucharistic Fast,* The Catholic University of America Canon Law Studies, n. 124, Washington, D. C.: The Catholic University of America Press, 1941.

Bernardus Papiensis, *Summa Decretalium,* ed. E. A. Laspeyres, Ratisbonae, 1860.

Cappello, Felix, *Tractatus Canonico-Moralis de Sacramentis,* 5 vols., Vol. I, *De Sacramentis in Genere, de Baptismo, Confirmatione et Eucharistiae,* 2. ed., Romae: Marietti, 1928.

Conway, William, *The New Law on the Eucharistic Fast,* Text, Translation, Commentary, 2. impression, Dublin: Brown & Nolan, 1955.

Coronata, Matthaeus Conte a, *De Nova Disciplina Ieiunii Eucharistici et De Missis Vespertinis,* Commentarium in Constitutionem *Christus Dominus* et in Instructionem Sancti Officii, diei 6 Ianuarii 1953, Romae: Officium Libri Catholici, 1955.

———, *Institutiones Iuris Canonici,* 2. ed., 5 vols. Tornacae-Romae: Marietti, 1939-1947.

Dix, Gregory, *The Treatise on the Apostolic Tradition of St. Hippolytus of Rome,* London: MacMillan, 1937.

Ford, John C. *The New Eucharistic Legislation,* A Commentary on the Apostolic Constitution *Christus Dominus* and on the Instruction of the Holy Office on the Discipline to be observed concerning the Eucharistic Fast, 2. ed. New York: Kenedy, 1955.

Hürth, Franciscus, *De Nova Disciplina Ieiunii Eucharistici,* Constitutio Apostolica *Christus Dominus* necnon Instructio SS. Officii (6 Ian. 1953), Textus et Commentarius, Romae: Pontificia Universitas Gregorians, 1953.

Jone, H., *Moral Theology,* Revised English Translation by Adelman, Westminster: Newman, 1953.

Kelly, Gerald, *Medico-Moral Problems in 5 Parts,* St. Louis: The Catholic Hospital Association of U. S. and Canada 1949-1954.

Michiels, Gommarus, *Normae Generales Iuris Canonici,* 2. ed., 2 vols., Parisiis-Tournai-Romae: Desclée, 1949.

Migne, J. R., *Patrologiae Cursus Completus,* Series Latina, 221 vols. Parisiis, 1844-1864.

Noldin, H.-Schmitt, A., *Summa Theologiae Moralis iuxta Codicem Iuris Canonici,* 3 vols., 26. ed. Oeniponte-Lipsiae: Feliciani Rauch, 1940-1941.

Ottaviani, Alaphridus. *Institutiones Iuris Publici Ecclesiastici,* 2 vols. in 1, Romae: Apud Aedes Facultatis Iuridicae ad S. Apollinaris, 1925.

Regatillo, E. F.-Zalba, M., *Theologiae Moralis Summa,* 3 vols., Matriti: Biblioteca de Autores Christianos, 1952-1954.

Schmidt, John Rogg, *The Principles of Authentic Interpretation in Canon 17 of the Code of Canon Law,* The Catholic University of America Canon Law Studies, n. 141, Washington, D. C.: The Catholic University of America Press, 1941.

Thomas Aquinas, St., *Summa Theologica,* 6 vols. Taurini: Marietti, 1926, Pars III, q. LXXX, a. 8.

Van Hove, A., *Commentarium Lovaniense in Codicem Iuris Canonici,* 1 vol. in 5 tomes, Tom. II, *De Legibus Ecclesiasticis,* Mechliniae-Romae: H. Dessain, 1930.

Walsh, John J., *The Jurisdiction of the Interritual Confessor in the United States and Canada,* The Catholic University of America Canon Law Studies, n. 320, Washington, D. C.: The Catholic University of America Press, 1950.

Articles

Bride, A., "Jeune Eucharistique," *Dictionnaire de Droit Canonique,* Fascicule XXXI (1954) 142-181.

———, "Jeune Eucharistique," *L'Ami du Clergé,* LXIII (1953), 192-208.

———, "Jeune Eucharistique," *L'Ami du Clergé,* LXIII (1953), 252-254.

———, "Jeune Eucharistique," *L'Ami du Clergé,* LXIII (1953), 321-335.

Connell, Francis J., "Answers to Questions," *The American Ecclesiastical Review,* CXXXVI (1957), 56.

Connell, Francis J., "The New Rules for the Eucharistic Fast," *The American Ecclesiastical Review,* CXXVIII (1953), 241-254.

Castellano, Mario, "Ad novam disciplinam circa ieiunium Eucharisticum commentarium," *Monitor Ecclesiasticus,* LXXVIII (1953), 386-410.

Castellano, Mario, "Ad novam disciplinam circa ieiunium Eucharisticum commentarium," *Monitor Ecclesiasticus,* LXXIX (1954), 19-50.

Danagher, John J., "Questions Answered," *The Homiletic and Pastoral Review,* LIV (1954), 1092-1094.

Delaney, Robert E., "The New Legislation on the Eucharistic Fast," *Conference Bulletin of the Archdiocese of New York,* XXXI (1954), 55-73.

Fanfani, P., "Alcuni dubbi intorno alla Costituzione 'Christus Dominus,'" *Palestra del Clero,* XXXII (1953), 145-149.

Felici, Pericles, "De nova ieiunii disciplina praecipue quoad fideles," *Apollinaris,* XXVIII (1955), 165-171.

Genicot, J.-Putz, J., "The Eucharistic Fast," *The Clergy Monthly,* XVII (1953), 45-55.

———. "The Eucharistic Fast," *The Clergy Monthly,* XVII (1953), 248-257.

———. "The Eucharistic Fast," *The Clergy Monthly,* XVII (1953), 281-288.

Key, Oren, W. "The Eucharistic Fast," *Theology Digest,* II (1954), 53-63.

Mahoney, E. J., "Questions and Answers," *The Clergy Review,* XXXVIII (1953), 160-168.

———, "Questions and Answers," *The Clergy Review,* XXXVIII (1953), 229-231.

———, "Questions and Answers," *The Clergy Review,* XXXVIII (1953), 358-367.

———, "Questions and Answers," *The Clergy Review,* XXXVIII (1953), 430-431.

Moriarty, Eugene J., "New Regulations on the Eucharistic Fast," *The Jurist,* XIV (1954), 1-31.

McCarthy, John, "The Eucharistic Fast," *The Irish Ecclesiastical Record,* 5. series, LXXXI (1954), 146-150.

McCarthy, John, "Notes and Queries," *The Irish Ecclesiastical Record,* 5. series, (1954), 418-420.

McReavy, L. L., "Correspondence," *The Clergy Review,* XXXVIII (1953), 575.

Onclin, William, "La Nouvelle Législation sur le Jêune Eucharistique," *Ephemerides Theologicae Lovaniensis,* XXIX (1953), 77-94.

Oldani, L., "La costituzione 'Christus Dominus', esposozione e commento," *Revista del Clero Italiano,* XXXIV (1953), 106-113.

Reed, John J., "Select Questions on the Eucharistic Fast," *Theological Studies,* XVI (1955), 30-76.

———, "Modified discipline of the Eucharistic Fast," *Theological Studies,* XIV (1953), 215-241.

Visser, J. "Nova legislatio canonica servanda quoad ieiunium Eucharisticum," *Euntes Docete,* VI (1953), 3-29.

Werts, Hilary R., "The Eucharistic Fast," *Review for Religious,* XII (1953), 305-316.

ALPHABETICAL INDEX

BIOGRAPHICAL NOTE

James Ruddy was born on April 18, 1916, in Kilfian, County Mayo, Ireland. He received his elementary education in the local National School. In 1933 he entered St. Muredach's College, the Minor Seminary, from which he was graduated in 1938. In September, 1938, he entered St. Peter's College, Wexford, where he was ordained to the Holy Priesthood on June 4, 1944, for the Diocese of Cheyenne. After serving as an assistant in several parishes of the Diocese of Cheyenne, he enrolled in the School of Canon Law at the Catholic University of America in the fall of 1954. He received the Baccalaureate in Canon Law in June, 1955, and the Licentiate in June, 1956.

CANON LAW STUDIES *

No. 375. Kelleher, Rev. Francis T., A.B., J.C.L., Judicial expenses.

No. 376. Bantigue, Rev. Pedro N., J.C.L., The Provincial Council of Manila of 1771.
(Its text followed by a commentary on *Actio II, De Episcopis*).

No. 377. Burns, Rev. Dennis J., J.C.L., Matrimonial indissolubility: contrary conditions.

No. 378. Deutsch, Rev. Bernard F., J.C.L., Jurisdiction of pastors in the external forum.

No. 379. Dunnivan, Rev. John P., A.B., J.C.L., Prejudicial attempts in pending litigation.

No. 380. Ernst, Rev. Albert C., A.B., J.C.L., Free admission to church for sacred rites.

No. 381. Frattin, Peter Louis, J.C.L., The matrimonial impediment of impotence: occlusion of the spermatic ducts and vaginismus.

No. 382. Henry, Rev. Charles W., O.S.R., A.B., S.T.L., J.C.L., Canonical relations between bishops and abbots at the beginning of the tenth century.

No. 383. Hoffman, Rev. Lawrence J., A.B., ST.B., J.C.L., Clergy conferences: Canon 131.

No. 384. Markham, Rev. James J., A.B., S.T.L., J.C.L., The Sacred Congregation of Seminaries and Universities of Studies.

No. 385. McGrath, Rev. John J., A.B., LL.B., J.C.L., A comparative study of crime and its imputability in ecclesiastical criminal law and in American criminal law.

No. 386. McGuire, Rev. James D., O.R.S.A., J.C.L., The postulancy.

No. 387. Munday, Rev. James E., J.C.L., Ecclesiastical Property in Australia and New Zealand.

No. 388. Murphy, Rev. Joseph P., A.B., J.C.L., The laws of the State of New York affecting church property.

No. 389. Pickard, Rev. Wm. M., J.C.L., Judicial experts: a source of evidence in ecclesiastical trials.

No. 390. Ruddy, Rev. James, J.C.L., The Apostolic Constitution *Christus Dominus:* text, translation and commentary, with short annotations on the Motu Proprio *Sacram Communionem.*

No. 391. Vanyo, Rev. Leo V., A.B., J.C.L., Requisites of intention in the reception of the sacraments.

* For a complete list of the available numbers of this series apply to the Catholic University of America Press, 620 Michigan Avenue, N.E., Washington (17), D. C., for a general catalog.

www.ingramcontent.com/pod-product-compliance
Lightning Source LLC
LaVergne TN
LVHW050215080826
844660LV00012B/412

* 9 7 8 0 8 1 3 2 2 5 5 0 0 *